Also edited by Archie Givens

Spirited Minds: African American Books
for Our Sons and Our Brothers

STRONG SOULS SINGING

STRONG SOULS SINGING

African American Books for Our Daughters and Our Sisters

Edited by
Archie Givens

Introduction by Marian Wright Edelman

W. W. Norton & Company
New York • London

Copyright © 1998 The Givens Foundation for
African American Literature
Introduction © 1998 by Marian Wright Edelman,
President, Children's Defense Fund
Illustrations © 1998 by William Raaum

The Archie and Phebe Mae Givens Foundation operates under the
name of the Givens Foundation for African American Literature.

Managing editors: Desnick & Nelson
Book design: Desnick & Nelson
Writers: Erin Sweet, Beth Desnick, Thea Nelson
Manufacturing by Quebecor Fairfield
The text of this book is composed in ITC New Baskerville, the display
set in Baker Signet, and initial caps are Desnick & Nelson Woodcut.

Library of Congress Cataloging-in-Publication Data

Strong souls singing : African American books for our daughters and
    our sisters / edited by Archie Givens ; introduction by Marian
    Wright Edelman.
        p. cm.
    Includes bibliographical references and index.
    ISBN 0-393-02745-7. — ISBN 0-393-31780-3 (pbk.)
    1. Afro-Americans—Juvenile literature—Bibliography.
    2. Children's literature, American—Afro-American authors—
Bibliography. 3. Afro-American women—Juvenile literature—
Bibliography. 4. Afro-American girls—Books and reading—
Bibliography. I. Givens, Archie, 1944–   .
    Z1361.N39S79 1998
    [E185]
    016.97304'96073—dc21   98-19854
                                                                   CIP

W. W. Norton & Company, Inc., 500 Fifth Avenue, New York, N.Y. 10110
http://www.wwnorton.com

W. W. Norton & Company Ltd., 10 Coptic Street, London WCIA IPU

1 2 3 4 5 6 7 8 9 0

To my mother, Phebe Mae Givens

For all our daughters and sisters

Contents

Why We Created This Book

I could not begin to reflect in words how much I have learned about other people, other places, other ideas from books. Apart from a love of reading, I have a profound respect for books, because I know what they have done to expand my world.

Thus, when the Archie Givens Sr. Collection of African American Literature was dedicated in memory of my father at the University of Minnesota eleven years ago, I knew that I wanted to make the literature available to the many students and scholars whose world would also be expanded by access to such rich material. Yet that was only the beginning.

In time, I came to envision how this body of literature could be important in ways I hadn't imagined. I came to appreciate its value to far more people than just those who were led to the literature to do research, or who happened to come upon the books in their search for other materials; I came to understand its power to open the hearts and minds of children and adults alike. I've watched this happen with my own daughters, whose love for books is as boundless as their souls.

With that inspiration, we at the Givens Foundation for African American Literature created *Strong Souls Singing: African American Books for Our Daughters and Our Sisters.* Along with its brother volume, *Spirited Minds: African American Books for Our Sons and Our Brothers*, it begins to show the breadth of genius in African American literature, to whet the appetites of new readers, and to give those who know the literature something to share with others. The books included here represent only a fraction of all that exist, but they help show the way to a universe of understanding and pleasure.

My purpose is to bring more attention to the great treasure that is African American literature. My dream is that by reading the books we will all learn something valuable about ourselves and about each other.

Archie Givens

Acknowledgments

So many dedicated people have brought their gifts to this book. My first thanks go to the thoughtful individuals whose early editorial input helped set the tone for *Strong Souls Singing*. These include Dr. Caroline Majak, Dave Jones, Jeanne Fox-Alston, and Ruby Anderson. Thanks also to Dr. Dianne Johnson-Feelings and Dr. Susan Watts-Taffe for providing comments on the list-in-progress.

My thanks to Caroline Knight and Margo Lloyd for their editorial insights, and for their expertise in literacy that kept us true to finding books to suit all ages. Thanks also to Miriam Butwin for her wonderfully knowledgeable and artful editing. My heartfelt gratitude to Erin Sweet for all of her tremendous work; she really knows how to sing.

There are so many others who have been at my side throughout this project. Thanks to my wife, Carol, for her love and support; to my sister, Roxanne, and my nieces, Rachael and Brittany; and to my own beautiful daughters, April and Sunny. My appreciation to the advisory board of the Givens Foundation for African American Literature for their dedication, to Angie Meshbesher for her encouragement, and to Janet Bisbee for her grantwriting assistance.

Finally, I want to express my warmest thanks to the Carolyn Foundation and the Cowles Media Foundation, who helped make this project possible, and to my friend Willis Bright of the Lilly Endowment, who was there at the very beginning.—A.G.

A Note about Reading Levels

Each of the five chapters in *Strong Souls Singing* begins with books for very young children, and progresses to books for high school and adult readers. The specific reading levels for each book appear at the end of each book description. In assigning these reading levels, we have analyzed the complexity of words and sentences, as well as subject matter.

Each book falls into one or more of five reading levels: **Picture Books**, **Grades 1 to 3**, **Grades 4 to 5**, **Grades 6 to 7**, **Grades 8 to 9**, and **Grade 10 to Adult**. When a book spans more than one of these reading levels, the skills of the reader should be at the level of the earliest grade stated, but the subject matter will also interest older readers. For instance, a book that is labeled "Grade 8 to Adult" is appropriate for anyone whose reading skills are at least those of an 8th grade student, but the contents of the book will appeal to adults as well.

Many picture books—illustrated books meant to be read to very young children—will also interest older children. The reading levels that follow some of the "Picture Book" designations refer to the grade at which the child will have the skills to read the book independently.

Lastly, when selecting a book to share with another—particularly a young person—look through it before making a final decision. This valuable step is one of the great joys of sharing books with others.

STRONG SOULS SINGING

Introduction
by Marian Wright Edelman

I was a blessed black girl. When I was a child, teachers in our segregated schools introduced us to "Lift Ev'ry Voice and Sing," the Negro national anthem by James Weldon Johnson, which reminded us of "the faith that the dark past has taught us and the hope that the present has brought us." At that time, we had two kinds of role models: those who achieved in the outside world—like my namesake, Marian Anderson, the first black woman to sing at the Metropolitan Opera—and those in our community who didn't have a lot of education or fancy clothes but who taught us by the special grace of their lives the message of all great faiths: that the Kingdom of God is within, in what you are, not what you have.

My mother and my father, who was a Baptist minister, were absolutely committed to their community and their family. I was fourteen years old the night my Daddy died. He had holes in his shoes but two children out of college, one in college, another in divinity school, and a vision that he was able to convey to me as he lay dying in an ambulance—that I, a young black girl, could be and do anything; that race and gender are shadows; and that character, self-discipline, determination, attitude, and service are the substance of life.

The home I grew up in had more books and magazines in it than clothes or luxuries, and I'm grateful for that.

Surrounding me from very early childhood were names like Langston Hughes, Mohandas Gandhi, Benjamin Mays, Howard Thurman, and W. E. B. Du Bois. My father valued reading almost as much as prayer, service, and work. The only time he would not assign chores for my brothers and sister and me was when we were reading—so we read a lot!

As a high school junior, for an oratory contest, I picked a speech Ralph Bunche gave at Fisk University in the 1940s entitled "The Barriers of Race Can Be Surmounted." As a teenager, I drew strength and inspiration from his words, and I still think back to that great speech on days when I need encouragement. How can we best teach our children about this great heritage—about the kings and queens of courage and achievement who helped make our land fairer for all Americans? How can our daughters learn to "stand tall," as Martin Luther King, Jr., said, if they don't know they stand on the shoulders of generations of women and men who endured and triumphed?

Reading is the answer. Books can show our children the strong, admirable black women and men who don't often appear on television, in a classroom setting, or on the nightly news. Through reading, we can be sure that our daughters and our sons grow up armed with knowledge and understanding of the power, idealism, faith, dedication, and perseverance of the women and men who fought and overcame some of the harshest atrocities ever perpetrated.

Books can bring our daughters the poetry of Phillis Wheatley, of Rita Dove, who was the nation's poet laureate, and of Gwendolyn Brooks, who, through her earlier work with the Library of Congress, helped pave the way for that great honor. Books can carry them around the world, with the literary genius of Nobel laureates Toni Morrison, Wole Soyinka, and Derek Walcott, and the eloquent words of black Nobel Peace laureates Ralph Bunche and Martin Luther King, Jr. Our daughters can fight and overcome slavery with Harriet Tubman, Sojourner Truth, and Frederick Douglass, and wrestle segregation to the ground with Fannie Lou Hamer and Rosa Parks.

Books can bring understanding: they can show how black girls and boys withstood bombings and fire hoses in Birmingham, mobs in Little Rock, Nashville, and Jackson, and taunts and jeers in Greensboro to overcome segregation and discrimination with moral courage. Our children can read Maya Angelou's and Mary McLeod Bethune's words telling them they can do anything and overcome any odds. They can pray with Paul Laurence Dunbar and James Weldon Johnson, or laugh with Langston Hughes's delightful character Simple.

It is time for all of us—parents, elders, preachers, teachers, and community leaders—to join together to guide our children to fill their minds through the power of reading. My work for the welfare of all our children brings me to many fronts: health care, education, child care, safety, and more. None of this would have happened had my parents not opened my world with reading. Whatever challenges or advantages children may experience, reading will anchor them to the faith and values that have sustained prior generations, while preparing them for their futures. Especially for girls, who face the double barriers of race and gender, reading shines a spotlight on women who have broken free from these restraints to reach for their dreams.

With *Strong Souls Singing*, Archie Givens has given us a place to start our children on this great path. If there is a black girl in your life, you need this book. If you are a parent, teacher, or adult who cares about our black youth, you need this book. Take a step: introduce a black child to the wonderful books listed here, read with her, and watch her mind open and her heart soar. Do it today.

History

Lift Ev'ry Voice and Sing
(1995)

James Weldon Johnson. Illustrations by Jan Spivey Gilchrist
Unpaged

This graceful picture book brings the spirit of the
song often called the "Negro National Anthem" to a new
generation. James Weldon Johnson cowrote this song with
his brother, J. Rosamond Johnson, at the turn of the
century. With rousing lines like "Let us march on till
victory is won," it filled the hearts and souls of all who
heard it, and won its place in African American history.
Gilchrist's dreamy, full-color illustrations fill each page. In
a note to readers, she explains what the song means to her
personally. *Lift Ev'ry Voice and Sing* is a treasure, bringing
home the song's uplifting message of faith and progress.

Picture Book to Adult

I Have a Dream

(1997)

Dr. Martin Luther King, Jr. Foreword by Coretta Scott King. Illustrations by fifteen Coretta Scott King Award and Honor Book artists

40 pages

On August 28, 1963, Martin Luther King, Jr., gave a speech that would forever alter the course of American history. His "I Have a Dream" speech stands as a symbol of the civil rights movement of the 1960s, and still resonates today in the continued struggle for equality. Here, readers will find the brilliant speech in its entirety. Fifteen great African American artists—Tom Feelings, Jan Spivey Gilchrist, Jerry Pinkney, Leo and Diane Dillon, and others—have taken a phrase of Dr. King's speech as the subject for a moving full-page illustration. These illustrations offer adults an opportunity to discuss Dr. King's speech with even very young children. Information about Dr. King, a brief foreword by his widow, Coretta Scott King, and comments by the artists round out this fabulous book. *I Have a Dream* will introduce all ages to the wisdom and eloquence of this American hero.

Picture Book to Adult

Witnesses to Freedom: Young People Who Fought for Civil Rights

(1993)

Belinda Rochelle

97 pages; illustrations

W*itnesses to Freedom* tells the fascinating stories of young people—some only six years old—who were involved in the battle for civil rights of the 1960s. At age sixteen, Barbara Johns helped organize a boycott to protest the horrible conditions at her segregated Virginia high school, which led to a lawsuit by the NAACP. Sheyann Webb was just eight years old when she began attending voting rights meetings and participating in rallies and marches. Young people were a crucial part of other important civil rights activities like the Freedom Rides, the March on Washington for Jobs and Freedom, and, of course, the Children's Crusade, in which thousands of young people marched in Birmingham, Alabama, in 1963. Photographs and personal profiles of those involved round out the book. *Witnesses to Freedom* offers inspiring testimony to the power young people have to shape history.

Grades 4 to 9

The Harlem Renaissance
(1998)
Veronica Chambers
128 pages

T his lively book introduces readers to the people and events that sparked the "explosion of creativity" in the 1920s known as the Harlem Renaissance. From A'Lelia Walker's fancy parties for writers and artists, to the concerns of everyday women and men living in Harlem, author Veronica Chambers offers a fascinating overview of the period. Readers will meet key players of the Renaissance, including W. E. B. Du Bois and Jessie Redmon Fauset, who jointly edited the NAACP's magazine *The Crisis*, in which many now-famous writers were first published. Also profiled are Langston Hughes, Countee Cullen, Claude McKay, and others. In a chapter titled "Renaissance Women," Chambers fills readers in on the prominent women of the period: the flamboyant Zora Neale Hurston, sculptor Augusta Savage, the mysterious Nella Larsen, the multitalented Gwendolyn Bennett. This introduction to one of the most exciting periods in American literary history sparkles with energy and wit, a fitting tribute to the legacy of the Harlem Renaissance.

Grade 4 to Adult

Get on Board: The Story of the Underground Railroad

(1993)

James Haskins

152 pages; illustrations

In this book James Haskins illuminates one of the most mysterious aspects of American history. Little is known about the earliest years of the Underground Railroad, including how the secret system of transporting slaves to freedom gained its name, but Haskins offers a few theories on the matter. By the 1830s, the Underground Railroad had become a formal network of stations, conductors, and routes leading North, often to Canada. Stations were the safe-houses in which fugitives were sheltered along their journey; they were equipped with special hiding spaces—sometimes even secret rooms and tunnels. Haskins introduces readers to conductors on the Underground Railroad, most notably the legendary Harriet Tubman. This book also includes spirituals; lines in these songs like "steal away, steal away to Jesus" held double meaning—the invitation to escape to freedom. Haskins's clear writing and the photos and drawings make this book a great introduction to a thrilling subject.

Grade 4 to Adult

"No one knows how many slaves tried to escape, or how many people tried to help them during the two-and-a-half centuries of slavery in the United States."

James Haskins
Get on Board: The Story of the Underground Railroad

The Best of The Brownies' Book

(1996)

Edited by Dianne Johnson-Feelings. Introduction by
Marian Wright Edelman

351 pages

his delightful book offers readers a fascinating
glimpse of what life was like for African American children
over seventy-five years ago. Published in 1920 and 1921,
The Brownies' Book was an offshoot of the popular NAACP
magazine *The Crisis,* and was written exclusively for young
people. The first magazine of its kind, it was edited by
W. E. B. Du Bois and Jessie Redmon Fauset, both prominent
figures in the blossoming Harlem Renaissance. Their
magazine featured short stories, biographies, poems, letters
from young people, illustrations, puzzles, and more. It also
highlighted the accomplishments of women and men of all
ages—urging young people to reach for the stars. With this
beautiful book, editor Dianne Johnson-Feelings brings
together the best pages from the magazine and sheds new
light on a rarely seen gem.

Grade 4 to Adult

Our Song, Our Toil: The Story of American Slavery as Told by Slaves
(1994)
Edited by Michele Stepto
95 pages

O*ur Song, Our Toil* is a brilliant showcase for the words of women and men who experienced the horrors of slavery firsthand. Editor Michele Stepto interweaves the stories of slaves with vivid descriptions of slavery. Harriet Jacobs speaks of her youngest years as a slave; Abream Scriven writes a desperate goodbye letter to his wife when his sale to another master is imminent; Mary Prince, a slave in Bermuda, describes the work she was forced to do in salt ponds from four in the morning until nine at night; and Frederick Douglass describes the moment he learned literacy was the key to freedom. A wide cross section of men and women tell their stories in this precious book; together their words form a powerful testimony to the resilience of the human spirit.

Grade 6 to Adult

Into the Fire: African Americans since 1970

(1996)
Robin D. G. Kelley
142 pages; illustrations

*I*nto the Fire is a sweeping look at recent events in African American history from noted historian Robin D. G. Kelley. The book opens with an overview of the politics of the 1970s, including the jailings of activists like Angela Davis and George Jackson, and follows the continuing fight for political power into the 1990s. Along the way, Kelley introduces readers to heroes as varied as Shirley Chisholm, the first African American woman to serve in the House of Representatives, the Reverend Jesse Jackson, and Anita Hill. Kelley delves into the deepening poverty strangling inner cities in the 1970s, and in a chapter titled "Living the Dream?" addresses the black middle class. The book also covers African American culture, highlighting accomplishments in the realms of music, film, television, and literature. Thought provoking and thorough, *Into the Fire* reviews the recent past and the issues that continue to shape young people's lives today.

Grade 8 to Adult

Go Down, Moses: A Celebration of the African-American Spiritual

(1998)

Richard Newman. Illustrations by Terrance Cummings.
Foreword by Cornel West
224 pages

This fabulous book showcases the beauty, wisdom, and history of the African American spiritual. In his informative introduction, author Richard Newman notes that spirituals reflect both African traditional life and the religious customs of the white American South. As such, what is today recognized as the first truly "American" music was created by enslaved African Americans. The words of two hundred spirituals cover the pages of this book. Each song is accompanied by fascinating bits of information that bring to life their drama and poignancy, and speak to their enduring influence in other areas of American culture and history. By turns hopeful, encouraging, and solemn, the spirituals often have double meanings, refering to escape plans, the miseries of slavery, and hope for freedom. *Go Down Moses* offers a warm introduction to a breathtaking subject.

Grade 8 to Adult

Warriors Don't Cry: A Searing Memoir of the Battle to Integrate Little Rock's Central High

(1994)

Melba Pattillo Beals

312 pages; illustrations

At the age of fifteen, Melba Pattillo became a self-described warrior. In 1957, she was one of the courageous "Little Rock Nine," the first students to integrate Central High School in Little Rock, Arkansas. Pattillo and the others faced extreme violence and unimaginable cruelty each day: bombings, physical abuse, and acid thrown in their eyes. Their bravery, and the ensuing power struggle between President Dwight D. Eisenhower and Governor Orval Faubus of Arkansas, captured the nation's attention. Melba Pattillo Beals draws on her diary and news reports to create this personal and stirring account of the battle. Her courage, bolstered by a strong religious faith and a supportive family, helped to change the face of our nation.

Grade 10 to Adult

The Middle Passage: White Ships/Black Cargo
(1995)

Tom Feelings. Introduction by John Henrik Clarke
Unpaged

At the opening of this book, Tom Feelings offers a moving and revealing explanation of why he created *The Middle Passage*, yet there is no way to prepare for the astonishing illustrations that follow. The Middle Passage refers to the journey slave ships made from West Africa to North and South America and the Caribbean. Thirty to sixty million Africans were subjected to this inhumane and unimaginable crime. Feelings's black-and-white illustrations convey the anguish of this experience, starting with the capture of the African prisoners, and continuing through image after image of the long journey itself. These pictures are at once horrifying and bewitching, yet it is precisely the mysterious beauty of the illustrations which—despite the horrific subject matter—conveys the enduring strength of the African spirit. *The Middle Passage* is a magnificent achievement that adults should page through hand-in-hand with young people.

Grade 10 to Adult

A Shining Thread of Hope: The History of Black Women in America

(1998)

Darlene Clark Hine and Kathleen Thompson

355 pages; illustrations

History comes alive in this comprehensive look at the lives of African American women over the centuries. Beginning in 1619 with the arrival of the first black woman in what would become the United States, and closing with an overview of today's achievements and challenges, Darlene Clark Hine and Kathleen Thompson have unearthed a multitude of facts about women both well known and obscure; they have written their stories with love and care. Drawing from a wide variety of sources, the authors cover the lives of black women during slavery, Reconstruction, the Great Depression, and the civil rights movement— survival techniques, motherhood, work—stressing the breadth of experiences. An impressive attention to detail runs throughout. Magnificently written and researched, this book is a must for every family.

Grade 10 to Adult

This Strange New Feeling

(1981)
Julius Lester
149 pages

Love and freedom—both are strange new feelings for the characters in this book. Inspired by true events in pre–Civil War America, these three stories take readers on a roller coaster of emotion, as young women and men fall in love, plan daring escapes, and fight for their freedom. Ras escapes North only to be captured by his master. Upon his return, he helps other slaves escape, earning the love of a special young woman. In another story, Maria falls in love with a free black man, who is able to "buy" her. Though she is legally his slave, she is able to live as a freedwoman until a tragic accident claims his life. Perhaps the most well known of these stories is that of Ellen and William Craft. To escape, Ellen poses as a sickly white man in need of a doctor, while her husband William pretends to be her slave. Each story, told with Julius Lester's characteristic zest, memorializes the bravery and resilience of these young women and men.

Grade 10 to Adult

Drama

A Raisin in the Sun: A Drama in Three Acts

(1959)

Lorraine Hansberry

142 pages

This magnificent play introduces readers to the Youngers—an extended family haunted and tortured by unfulfilled dreams. As the play opens, the Youngers await a $10,000 check in the mail. The check is an insurance settlement arising from the death of Lena Younger's husband. All have their eyes on the money, especially Lena's grown son, Walter Lee, whose plans for investing the money are dubious and risky. Yet, the battle over money is about much more than greed; it is the catalyst for a confrontation about the family members' conflicting and unachieved dreams. *A Raisin in the Sun* was the first play by an African American woman to be produced on Broadway. With intensity and dignity, it captures the dynamics of a family in the midst of a painful crisis.

Grade 8 to Adult

Fires in the Mirror: Crown Heights, Brooklyn and Other Identities
(1993)
Anna Deavere Smith. Foreword by Cornel West
141 pages

I n August 1991 in a Brooklyn neighborhood, a black child was killed by a driver in the motorcade of a Jewish religious leader. Later that day, a young Jewish man was killed in retaliation, and the ensuing riot lasted for three days. Anna Deavere Smith gives voice to both sides of the Crown Heights conflict in her one-woman drama, *Fires in the Mirror*. Using quotations from twenty-six interviews she conducted, Smith exposes the thoughts and feelings that burst from this charged event. Those interviewed range from neighborhood residents and rappers to authors and activists, as Smith believes that "everyone, in a given amount of time, will say something that is like poetry." The result is a rhythmic and thought-provoking piece that eloquently confronts the difficult issue of racial conflict.

Grade 8 to Adult

Pretty Fire

(1995)

Charlayne Woodard

53 pages

With *Pretty Fire*, Charlayne Woodard has crafted an entertaining autobiographical one-woman play based on her early years in Albany, New York. Beginning with her dramatic and near-fatal entrance into the world, Woodard takes us through her eleventh year when she satisfies Grandmama's second "dying wish" and joyously raises the roof at a Sunday service by singing a spirited solo— foretelling her successful career in the theater years later. In an earlier scene, Charlayne and her younger sister Allie visit their grandparents in Georgia. The girls' innocent love for Dixie is chilled when they witness a night ride of the Ku Klux Klan, and the subsequent burning of a cross— a "pretty fire" to young Charlayne, until she is set straight by Grandmama. These touching and sometimes painful recollections capture a childhood filled with love, humor, and warmth. Young readers and adults alike will be charmed by this lively account of a young performer's early life.

Grade 8 to Adult

Wines in the Wilderness: Plays by African American Women from the Harlem Renaissance to the Present

(1990)
Edited by Elizabeth Brown-Guillory
251 pages

This collection features thirteen plays by nine African American women playwrights of the twentieth century. From the early plays of Marita Bonner and Eulalie Spence to more recent works by Sonia Sanchez and Sybil Klein, readers are given a rich sampling of these gifted writers. Each playwright's section is preceded by an informative biography and brief descriptions of the plays. While they vary greatly in setting and subject matter—Georgia Douglas Johnson's *Blueblood* occurs during the Civil War, and Alice Childress's *Wine in the Wilderness* is set during a riot in Harlem in 1964—they all portray strong heroines who speak powerfully about the African American female experience. This book offers a rare opportunity to explore the talents of great black women playwrights.

Grade 10 to Adult

Mojo and String: Two Plays by Alice Childress

(1971)

Alice Childress

50 pages

Alice Childress's great talent for capturing the human spirit is showcased in this pair of one-act plays. In *Mojo: A Black Love Story*, Irene pays a visit to her ex-husband, Teddy, and reveals that she is very ill and awaiting surgery. In the course of their conversation, which is peppered with humor and sorrow, the couple rediscovers their true fondness for each other. An adaptation of a short story by Guy de Maupassant, *String* takes place during a neighborhood picnic where a group of people are poking fun at harmless, eccentric old Joe. When an obnoxious cafe owner who's been boasting about his wealth notices his wallet is missing, old Joe is unfairly accused of theft. The unfounded prejudice that old Joe faces from these well-to-do people accentuates their nastiness in contrast to his gentle, if odd, behavior. These two plays, strikingly different, but equally fascinating, offer a sparkling introduction to the works of Alice Childress.

Grade 10 to Adult

Flyin' West

(1995)
Pearl Cleage
80 pages

Following the Civil War, a great number of African American homesteaders, many of them women, left the South to seek freedom from racial violence and build new lives for themselves in the Western states. Pearl Cleage's *Flyin' West* , set in 1898, introduces us to four strong women who are struggling to hold on to the land they love in the all-black town of Nicodemus, Kansas. They have big plans for the town—a school, a post office, an expanded church, a book publishing company—but are fighting against the onslaught of white investors who want to snatch up the land. When Minnie, the youngest of the group, arrives in Nicodemus with her abusive and arrogant new husband, the women are forced into action to save Minnie's life and to protect their land. *Flyin' West* is a gripping play that speaks to the power and determination of these trailblazing pioneers.

Grade 10 to Adult

Black Girl: A Play in Two Acts
(1971)
J. E. Franklin
50 pages

B *lack Girl* tells the story of Billie Jean, a seventeen-year-old girl who lives with her grandmother and mother, Mama Rosie, in an oppressive household in a small Texas town. A high school dropout and aspiring dancer, Billie Jean finds no support for her talent from her mother or from older stepsisters who frequent the house. Mama Rosie, who sees her own failures mirrored in her daughters, withholds her affection from them, transferring it instead to troubled young women she takes in as boarders. To her daughters' disgust, she idolizes Netta, a former boarder who has been away at college. When the eldest daughters hear of Netta's upcoming visit to their mother, they plan to bully her, and Billie Jean, who is particularly jealous of Netta, is easily swayed to take part in their plot. The resulting violent encounter exposes the stepsisters' dishonesty toward Billie Jean, and prompts her to move out of the house to join Netta, and pursue her dreams. Sharply written, *Black Girl* is a powerful telling of a young woman's will to improve her life against all odds.

Grade 10 to Adult

MAMA ROSIE: Girl, I don't wanna hear nothing about no darn dancing . . . I done told you that old mess you doing ain't nothing.

J. E. Franklin
Black Girl

The Alexander Plays

(1992)

Adrienne Kennedy. Foreword by Alisa Solomon

107 pages

he Alexander Plays is a collection of three one-act plays and a monologue by Obie-award-winning playwright Adrienne Kennedy. The main character in these dramas is Suzanne Alexander, a prominent African American writer who speaks of her disturbing past in a hauntingly graceful voice. In *She Talks to Beethoven*, Alexander carries on a conversation with the spirit of the composer while she is in Ghana, awaiting news of her husband, David, who is feared dead. *The Ohio State Murders* recounts Alexander's difficult college years and the subsequent murders of her twin daughters. *The Film Club* and *The Dramatic Circle* take place in London as Alexander and her sister-in-law wait for word about David, who is missing once again. Kennedy's dream-like recounting of Alexander's memories—throughout which poetic, literary, and musical works are beautifully interwoven—creates a dramatic contrast to the larger issues of race, politics, and gender that she captures here.

Grade 10 to Adult

for colored girls who have considered suicide / when the rainbow is enuf: a choreopoem

(1977)
Ntozake Shange
64 pages

Influential and provocative, *for colored girls* is a cross section of poetry, dance, and drama featuring a cast of seven women, each identified by a color rather than a name, and each from a different part of the country. In a series of poem-like speeches that brilliantly twist the rules of "proper" grammar, these women tell of dancing and youth, men and love, infidelity and betrayal, abortion and rape, and extreme violence. What rings through the pain is an affirmation of the powerful bond they share with each other as black women. The lady in brown ends the play, saying, "& this is for colored girls who have considered suicide / but are movin to the ends of their own rainbows." *for colored girls* soars with its vision of women healing women and creating a brighter future, one in which all women recognize—and protect—their inner beauty.

Grade 10 to Adult

Novels
and
Short Stories

Just Us Women

(1982)

Jeannette Caines. Illustrations by Pat Cummings
Unpaged

Just *Us Women* tells the tale of a road trip that all children will enjoy. When a young girl takes a driving trip with her Aunt Martha, she delights in stopping whenever she sees something that strikes her fancy. Expressive illustrations by Pat Cummings show aunt and niece pulling over to browse at yard sales, buy fresh fruit from farmers, take pictures, and even walk in the rain. Freed from the practical but sometimes disapproving glances of the rest of the family, they can stop as often as they want—or even eat breakfast at night. But for this young girl, the best part of the trip is spending time alone with her favorite aunt. As she puts it, "No boys, no men—just us women."

Picture Book to Grade 3

Amazing Grace
(1991)

Mary Hoffman. Illustrations by Caroline Binch
Unpaged

Amazing Grace lives for storytelling of any kind. She
loves books, the stories culled from her grandmother's
memory, and the tales she creates in her own mind.
Whatever the story, Grace acts it out, always giving herself
the starring role. So when her teacher announces Grace's
class will perform *Peter Pan*, she knows only one role will
do for her. At first, some of her classmates don't agree. Raj
tells Grace that a girl can't be Peter Pan, and Natalie
whispers to her that she can't play Peter Pan because "he
isn't black." That day, Grace comes home upset, and her
mother and grandmother set about to show her she can't
let such nonsense hold her back. Wise words and a special
trip with her grandmother convince Grace to fight for the
role she really wants. Caroline Binch's full-color illustrations
draw out Grace's creative, dramatic personality in this
thoughtful story that adults will enjoy sharing with young
children, and talking about for months to come.

Picture Book to Grade 3

One of Three

(1991)

Angela Johnson. Illustrations by David Soman
Unpaged

H aving two older sisters means seeing the world in terms of threesomes for the young girl in this charming picture book. She's "one of the three" who have long brown hair and brown eyes; who walk to school together; who enjoy riding on the subway and in taxicabs with their family. No matter what the activity, it is usually measured in terms of "Eva, Nikki, and me" for this little girl. So when her sisters sometimes want to leave her at home, life can seem pretty lonely, until her mother and father show her she's part of another threesome altogether: "Mama, Daddy, and me." Words and illustrations work together in this book to highlight the joys and frustrations of being the youngest—of three.

Picture Book to Grade 3

Julius
(1993)
Angela Johnson. Illustrations by Dav Pilkey
Unpaged

In this imaginative picture book by Angela Johnson, a young girl named Maya and a gigantic Alaskan pig—Julius—teach each other some important lessons. A present from Maya's grandfather who winters in Alaska, Julius arrives in a huge crate with the promise that he will teach her about having fun and sharing. Although her parents aren't exactly thrilled, it's love at first sight for Maya. At first, Julius causes a commotion in the household, eating too much food, playing loud music, watching TV too late, and leaving his towels on the floor. But he's a great companion for Maya, thrilling her with his dog imitations and teaching her to dance to jazz records. In turn, Maya teaches Julius some manners, and her eccentric grandfather's promise comes true after all. Clever, vibrant illustrations by Dav Pilkey will charm readers of all ages with their comic portrayal of an enormous pink pig as family member. *Julius* is pure delight.

Picture Book to Grade 3

Tar Beach

(1991)
Written and illustrated by Faith Ringgold
Unpaged

Artist Faith Ringgold takes flight with this imaginative picture book about eight-year-old Cassie Louise Lightfoot. It's 1939 and Cassie lives with her family in Harlem, where her father is a builder and the rooftop of their apartment is their "tar beach." From her rooftop perch, Cassie soars in her mind, flying over bridges and office buildings, and the ice-cream factory. Cassie rules that everything she flies over, she owns, and with this new power she can be free forever. But what she wants more than anything is to help her father get into the union—which closes out anyone who is not white—so that he can always have work and the family can be secure. The brilliantly colored illustrations bring Cassie's dreaming to life. Faith Ringgold has created a book that will delight parents and children alike.

Picture Book to Grade 3

Uncle Jed's Barbershop
(1993)

Margaree King Mitchell. Illustrations by James Ransome
Unpaged

I n this heartwarming picture book, Margaree King
Mitchell has created a loving story about family and the
virtue of never giving up on your dreams. Just big enough
to be swept off the ground and hugged in the big arms of
her favorite great-uncle, Jedediah Johnson, a young girl
tells the story of her uncle's unending dream of opening
his own barbershop in the South in the early 1900s. Twice
he is able to save nearly enough money to reach his dream,
and then something happens to swallow it up: the first
time, he gives his savings to the family for the girl's emer-
gency surgery; the second time, the Great Depression hits.
Finally, Uncle Jed's dream is fulfilled, to the great joy of all
the people he shared his kindness with over the years.
James Ransome's wonderful full-page illustrations glow
with the warmth and kindness in this story.

Picture Book to Grade 3

I Want to Be

(1993)

Thylias Moss. Illustrations by Jerry Pinkney

Unpaged

A simple question sends a young girl on a journey of the imagination in this wonderful picture book by poet Thylias Moss. When her neighbors ask what she wants to be, this young girl thinks about it so long that they get impatient, and she promises to give them the answer the next day. During an unhurried walk home, she lets her thoughts wander as she considers the matter. "I danced until I was dizzy and the sky turned into a lake," she says, and "I double-dutched with strands of rainbow." Playful full-color illustrations by Jerry Pinkney beautifully convey these magical daydreams. By the time she arrives at home, the girl knows that she wants to be "big, but not so big that a mountain or a mosque or a synagogue seems small." Likewise, she wants to be "fast but not so fast that lightning seems slow." Lyrical and invigorating, *I Want to Be* invites young readers to open their minds to the infinite possibilities of the imagination.

Picture Book to Grade 5

Cornrows

(1979)

Camille Yarbrough. Illustrations by Carole Byard

Unpaged

When Shirley Ann, better known to her family as Sister, comes inside from playing to find Great-Grammaw braiding her mother's hair in cornrows, she and her little brother are bursting with questions. As they settle into place to have their own hair braided, their mother and Great-Grammaw tell them, in a mixture of song and spoken words, about the history behind their cornrows— a hairstyle called *suku*, which means basket in the African language Yoruba. Sister learns that cornrows were important symbols of African cultures, worn "from Senegal to Somali," and that people from different clans and villages could be identified by the style of their hair. Dramatic black-and-white illustrations by Carole Byard provide a stunning backdrop to this story told from Sister's youthful perspective. Blending history, song, and tradition in its portrayal of a loving family, *Cornrows* is a delight to read and share.

Picture Book to Grade 5

Sweet Clara and the Freedom Quilt

(1993)

Deborah Hopkinson. Illustrations by James Ransome

Unpaged

Told in the strong, willful voice of Sweet Clara, this picture book will captivate readers of all ages with its vivid description of her escape from slavery, and how she helped others do the same. Clara wasn't quite twelve years old when she was taken away from her mother to work on another plantation, but she never gave up her dream to be reunited with her. As a seamstress in the Big House, Clara began to hear talk about the Underground Railroad and running away, and realized if slaves had a map, it would be much easier to escape. That was when she began hiding away pieces of cloth for what would become the freedom quilt, a secret map of the area, including the Ohio River, which led to freedom in the North. Full-color illustrations by James Ransome highlight Clara's creativity and determination to be free. A delightful book to share with young people, *Sweet Clara and the Freedom Quilt* offers a unique gateway into African American history.

Picture Book, Grades 4 to 7

Mufaro's Beautiful Daughters: An African Tale

(1987)

Written and illustrated by John Steptoe

Unpaged

Author John Steptoe's lush, finely detailed illustrations make this picture book based on an African folktale sing with beauty. Mufaro is a villager, happy and proud of his two beautiful daughters, Manyara and Nyasha. Yet one crucial detail escapes Mufaro's attention: only one of his daughters is the kind person she appears to be. It's no secret to the other villagers that Manyara is greedy, jealous, and mean-spirited, taunting her kind sister Nyasha behind their father's back. When a messenger brings word that the king is inviting "the most worthy and beautiful daughters in the land" to his kingdom so that he may marry, Manyara exposes her true colors, learning a painful lesson about how to treat others. Young readers will be thrilled as Nyasha's good deeds are handsomely rewarded. With visual details inspired by the ruins of an ancient city in present-day Zimbabwe, *Mufaro's Beautiful Daughters* presents a classic theme in a gorgeous package.

Picture Book, Grades 4 to 7

Koya DeLaney and the Good Girl Blues

(1992)
Eloise Greenfield
124 pages

Sixth-grader Koya DeLaney is a riot. She loves to laugh and she has a knack for making others laugh with her. Koya's clever, funny personality makes her popular with her sister Loritha and their best friend Dawn, but sometimes it doesn't do her any favors. Koya can't stand conflict. In her eyes, "People look ugly when they're mad, and they act ugly, too!" Whenever things get uneasy, Koya cracks a joke, and usually everyone forgets what they were so upset about. But when Koya's cousin Del, a popular musician with a hit song, comes to town, a conflict explodes between Dawn and Loritha that even Koya's joking can't subdue. Koya learns that sometimes people have to confront others and express anger in order to stand up for themselves and for what's right. Young readers will identify with Koya's struggle to find her voice in this upbeat novel.

Grades 4 to 7

"*Children were bouncing in their seats. Sound was bouncing off the walls. The room was rocking.*"

Eloise Greenfield
Koya DeLaney and the Good Girl Blues

Yolonda's Genius

(1995)

Carol Fenner

211 pages

Fiercely intelligent, seemingly tough-as-nails fifth-grader Yolonda uses book and street smarts to protect herself and her shy six-year-old brother Andrew. Tall and powerfully built, Yolonda felt she had everything under control back in Chicago. But now, in the small town of Grand River, Michigan, everything is different, even Andrew. Just as Yolonda discovers that her brother is a musical genius who can effortlessly mimic the sounds around him on his harmonica, something stops him. Yolonda knows that she has to get an adult to recognize his talent, so it doesn't go wasted, but nobody else seems to understand her unique little brother, not even their well-meaning mother. Yolonda's solution is gutsy and calculated, but if anyone can pull it off, she can. Readers will be relieved to see that by the novel's end, she starts working out some of her own problems, too. In this beautifully written novel Carol Fenner has created two characters who seem to jump off the page and into the reader's imagination.

Grades 4 to 7

Cousins

(1990)

Virginia Hamilton

125 pages

Cousins explores the most painful summer Cammy has ever known. The eleven-year-old has some special people in her life: her ninety-four-year-old Gram Tut, her sixteen-year-old brother Andrew, and, of course, her mother. But she also has some enemies—and cousin Patty Ann tops the list. Patty Ann flaunts her grades, popularity, and expensive clothes until Cammy gets so mad she wishes her cousin would die. Throughout the summer in their small Ohio town, this rivalry between cousins grows vicious, as each girl wounds the other where it hurts the most. The novel takes an even darker turn when Cammy witnesses a tragic accident that claims Patty Ann's life. She remembers the wish she made in anger, and feels responsible. Visions of Patty Ann haunt Cammy and she sinks into a deep depression, but eventually her mother, Andrew, and Gram Tut help her deal with her grief, regret, and sorrow. This tender novel will move all readers, and will ring true for anyone who has experienced an unexpected loss.

Grades 4 to 7

Yellow Bird and Me

(1986)

Joyce Hansen

155 pages

For eleven-year-old Doris, life just isn't the same without her best friend Amir, who has moved away. As the novel opens, Doris just wants to be alone, doubting that any of the kids on her block of 163rd Street in the Bronx could fill his shoes. But that clowning, crazy Yellow Bird, known to most adults as James Towers, just won't stop pestering her to help him with his schoolwork. Yellow Bird always disrupts their sixth grade class with his foolishness, and that's why Doris thinks he's failing, at least at first. The more she helps him, the more she gets to know the real Yellow Bird—a pleasant surprise. Her tutoring reveals another surprise: Yellow Bird acts up in class to hide a reading problem that even their teacher doesn't know about. The true meaning of friendship flows through this tender book, Joyce Hansen's second novel about the kids of 163rd Street.

Grades 4 to 7

Running Girl: The Diary of Ebonee Rose

(1997)
Sharon Bell Mathis
60 pages; illustrations

leven-year-old Ebonee Rose, who goes by the name E. R., lives for running. This book takes the form of her diary, where she writes to pump herself up for the upcoming All-City Track Meet. Here, she writes about runners who inspire her and push her to do her best. The words and photographs of Florence Griffith Joyner, Wilma Rudolph, Jackie Joyner-Kersee, Wyomia Tyus, Mae Faggs and others—all African American women—are sprinkled throughout the diary. E. R. also writes about the runners in her own life, like Queenie, a talented new girl on the team she doesn't quite understand. Jam-packed with facts about track and field, *Running Girl* introduces readers to a girl whose dedication and boundless spirit are incredibly inspiring—not just for runners, but for anyone with a dream.

Grades 4 to 7

Willie Bea and the Time the Martians Landed

(1983)

Virginia Hamilton

208 pages

T welve-year-old Willie Bea Mills has had an eventful day visiting with her relatives, having her palm read by glamorous Aunt Leah, and fighting with her mean cousin, Little—but she can't even begin to imagine the night that's to come. It's October 30, 1938, and Willie is dressing her little brother and sister for "the night of beggars" in the rural farmland of Ohio, when Aunt Leah comes tearing into the house weeping about Martians. "Heard it on the radio. The world. *The-world-is-coming-to-an-end!*" she shrieks, instantly turning Willie Bea's world upside down. As the night goes on, everyone—including the adults—becomes increasingly frightened and even hysterical. The Martians become all too real when Willie Bea decides to investigate the rumors herself, and takes off in the dark. Based on the real-life broadcast of Orson Welles's radio-play that was mistaken for a news broadcast, *Willie Bea and the Time the Martians Landed* is a rich, humorous portrait of a most unusual day and night.

Grades 4 to 9

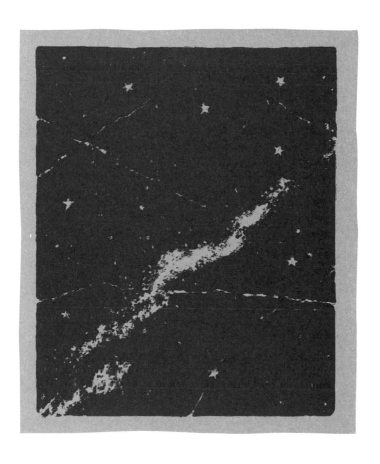

"*Up there was a wide, deep universe. It looked distant, up there. It looked dark, even though there were lots of stars. And smoky, way up there, too.*"

Virginia Hamilton
Willie Bea and the Time the Martians Landed

Hold Fast to Dreams

(1995)

Andrea Davis Pinkney

106 pages

As *Hold Fast to Dreams* opens, twelve-year-old Deirdre "Camera Dee" Willis is sitting in a dark, unfamiliar kitchen, worrying about her first day of school in overwhelmingly white Wexford, Connecticut. Her family has just moved from Redmond Avenue in Baltimore, where Dee loved her double-dutch team, the Jumpin' Jive Five, and taking pictures of familiar sights. In Wexford, there aren't any double-dutch teams—instead, all the kids play lacrosse, a game Dee can do without. At first, Dee thinks she's the only one in her close-knit family having trouble adjusting to Wexford. But once she shares her feelings with them and finds out what they're going through, too, she actually begins to notice some good things about Wexford: the beautiful doe she saw on her way to school; that girl, Web, who wants to be her friend; and even the talent show assembly that she keeps hearing about. Thoughtful and easy-to-read, *Hold Fast to Dreams* urges young people to remain true to themselves.

Grades 4 to 9

The Shimmershine Queens
(1989)
Camille Yarbrough
142 pages

Nobody can outdo you when yo get-up gift workin and you
get the shimmershine." These words of encouragement come
from Angie Peterson's Great Cousin Seatta, who tells Angie
that the shimmershine is that warm, happy feeling a
person gets when she loves herself and tries her best.
Angie gets the shimmershine feeling when she daydreams
to forget her worries and problems. She wonders if her
father is coming back, and if her depressed mother is
going to get better, and she worries about the teasing she
endures at school and about her dangerous neighborhood.
Angie carries a heavy load of problems, but armed with
some facts about African American history from Cousin
Seatta and the support of her best friend Michelle, Angie
vows to stand up for herself and get the shimmershine
whenever she can. When her class performs a play about
Africa, it's time for Angie to put this new knowledge and
self-esteem to work. This moving story will have readers
rooting for Angie and Michelle, the shimmershine queens.

Grades 4 to 9

Her Stories: African American Folktales, Fairy Tales, and True Tales

(1995)

Virginia Hamilton. Illustrations by Leo and Diane Dillon
112 pages

Trickster rabbits, talking eggs, glowing fairies, and many other fantastic creatures fill this book of folklore about women. Acclaimed author Virginia Hamilton can remember her own mother telling her several of the tales in this book, which is dedicated to "our mothers and grandmothers, aunts and great-aunts." *Her Stories* ranges wide, from true stories to legends like that of the seven-foot-tall Annie Christmas, and even to the supernatural story of a young girl named Malindy who outsmarts an inexperienced devil by giving him the sole of her shoe, rather than her soul. Hamilton gives readers background information about each tale's origin, explaining how it fits into African American folklore. Breathtaking full-color illustrations by Leo and Diane Dillon highlight the drama and mystery of each tale. *Her Stories* is a glowing tribute to all African American women—past, present, and future.

Grade 4 to Adult

Tituba of Salem Village

(1964)

Ann Petry

254 pages

lectrifying and riveting, this book is a fictional tale based on the true story of Tituba, one of the first women to be accused in the Salem Witch Trials of 1692. Tituba and her husband, slaves from Barbados, were sold to a stern minister who eventually settled in Salem Village, Massachusetts. When a group of young women in the community, including the minister's daughter and orphaned niece, become fascinated with trances and fortune-telling, they set in motion a tragic chain of events. Petry masterfully portrays the resulting atmosphere of paranoia and hysteria, as the young women start having fits in which they scream, dance, roll their eyes, and loll their tongues out of their mouths. Caught in the middle of this ruckus is the kind and intelligent Tituba. Petry shows readers that, ironically, these virtues lead to her downfall in this twisted community. *Tituba of Salem Village* offers a brilliant, yet easy-to-read commentary on a society built upon suspicion and fear.

Grade 4 to Adult

Song of the Trees
(1975)

Mildred D. Taylor. Illustrations by Jerry Pinkney
48 pages

Set in Depression-era rural Mississippi, this short
novel pits the intelligence and bravery of the Logan family
against the brute force of white racism. For eight-year-old
Cassie Logan, the soft rustling branches of the giant trees
on her family's precious land sing a special song. But the
day she finds white "X" marks painted on many of their
trunks, her beloved trees stand silent. Cassie and her
brothers overhear a white man's plan to force her grandmother to let him cut down these trees, so he can sell
them to lumbermen. Cassie's father, who is working on
the railroad in Louisiana, is sent for immediately, but
meanwhile, Cassie and her brothers face violence in their
unsuccessful fight to save their trees. In the end, Cassie
witnesses her father take a bold, calculated risk to save the
remainder of the forest from the hands of the greedy white
men. *Song of the Trees* is the first of several breathtaking
novels by Mildred Taylor.

Grade 4 to Adult

Second Daughter: The Story of a Slave Girl
(1996)
Mildred Pitts Walter
214 pages

History and imagination intersect in this fascinating book by Mildred Pitts Walter. Elizabeth Freeman, a slave better known to whites as "Mum Bett," successfully sued her master in 1781, arguing that the newly created Massachusetts Constitution guaranteed her freedom. This historic lawsuit ended slavery in the state. While this amazing action has been recorded, not much else is known about Elizabeth Freeman, beyond the fact she had a husband and a sister. *Second Daughter* begins where the history books leave off, offering readers a fictional version from the perspective of Elizabeth's younger sister, Aissa, whose name means "second daughter." "I must tell my story," she says as the book begins, "for I, too, have a life. I, too, have a name."

Grade 4 to Adult

Last Summer with Maizon

(1990)

Jacqueline Woodson

105 pages

A s this stunning novel begins, eleven-year-old Margaret feels as if she's "balancing between today and tomorrow." Her dad is going back to the hospital for more tests on his heart, and her best friend Maizon is waiting to hear if she's been accepted into an exclusive private school in Connecticut. When Margaret's worst fears come true—her father dies, and Maizon leaves for the prep school—nothing is the same on Madison Street in Brooklyn. Margaret's got her mother, baby brother, and neighbors to lean on for support, but she still feels all alone. When Maizon doesn't answer Margaret's letters, she's afraid that they've become "old friends," rather than the best friends she thought they'd always be. Yet life continues despite Margaret's grief, and when her teacher enters a poem she wrote about her father and Maizon in a citywide contest, Margaret feels good for the first time in what feels like forever. In *Last Summer with Maizon*, author Jacqueline Woodson brilliantly portrays a young girl finding strength deep within herself during a very painful period.

Grade 4 to Adult

The Friends

(1973)

Rosa Guy

203 pages

Fourteen-year-old Phyllisia Cathy has absolutely no desire to become friends with Edith Jackson—at least at first. She turns up her nose at Edith's unkempt appearance, and even ignores her attempts at friendliness. Phyllisia, who has just moved to Harlem, gets taunted because of her West Indian accent and bullied because she's always trying to prove her intelligence. One day, after Phyllisia has been beaten up by a classmate, Edith stands up to the bullies, and a unique friendship begins. Phyllisia soon finds out that Edith's mom died a few years earlier and her silent father seems nonexistent, leaving Edith to serve as a parent and provider to her four younger sisters. Financially, Phyllisia's family is much better off, but she constantly struggles with her sometimes cruel, always controlling father. For a time, Phyllisia and Edith help each other, until their differences and troubles threaten to separate them forever. Young people will be drawn to this intelligent novel—one that remains meaningful today, twenty-five years after it was first published.

Grade 6 to Adult

I Thought My Soul Would Rise and Fly: The Diary of Patsy, a Freed Girl

(1997)

Joyce Hansen

202 pages

I'm *so frightened my heart is dancing a reel in my chest.*"
So begins the secret diary kept by young Patsy in the first
days after the Civil War. Because she stutters and walks with
a limp, most everyone on the plantation—black and
white—has dismissed Patsy as dim-witted. No one would
guess she taught herself how to read and write by listening
in on the white children's lessons. Although slavery is
legally over, life doesn't change overnight for Patsy and the
other ex-slaves—and if the plantation owner has his way, it
never will. When shy, quiet Patsy reveals her secret skill to
the other ex-slaves, she finds herself feeding the fire of
true freedom by teaching others how to read. Author Joyce
Hansen has created a true heroine in Patsy, whose courage
will keep readers glued to the page.

Grade 6 to Adult

Toning the Sweep
(1993)

Angela Johnson

103 pages

Emmie's Grandmama Ola has her hair in dreadlocks and drives a beautifully kept 1964 Buick convertible at lightning speed through the desert. But she's dying of cancer. Fourteen-year-old Emmie and her mother have come to help Ola say goodbye to her eccentric desert community; she will live her final days with them in their Cleveland home. Emmie has always loved visiting her free-spirited grandmother and her equally colorful circle of friends. On this trip, she's videotaping everything in sight as a remembrance for Ola—and herself. Moving preparations remind Emmie's mother and grandmother of their move from Alabama to the desert in 1964, just days after the brutal, race-driven murder of Emmie's grandfather, and cause Emmie to ponder the man she never had the chance to meet. The voices of all three generations of women color this heartfelt novel, offering a uniquely beautiful perspective on saying goodbye.

Grade 6 to Adult

Annie John

(1985)
Jamaica Kincaid
148 pages

M ore than slightly conceited, very intelligent, and
equally mischievous, the likable Annie John is ten years old
when the novel opens, and is going through a period of
intense curiosity about death—even secretly attending
funerals in her efforts to discover its mysteries. Annie
describes a childhood on the island of Antigua spent at the
side of her mother, whom she adored. "It was in such a
paradise that I lived," she says, until soon after her twelfth
birthday, when her mother decides she is now a "young
lady," a mysterious label with a whole new set of rules for
Annie. Suddenly, Annie feels she's been completely cut off
from her mother's affection and love. Author Jamaica
Kincaid portrays this bewildering and painful passage into
adolescence with her characteristic wit, capturing the
emotional essence of childhood events, and retelling them
with a surprising and delightful matter-of-factness. *Annie
John*'s clever exploration of the mother-daughter relationship, written with beautiful simplicity, will charm young
readers and adults alike.

Grade 6 to Adult

Another Way to Dance

(1996)
Martha Southgate
179 pages

Fourteen-year-old Vicki Harris has a passionate secret crush on Mikhail Baryshnikov, or Misha, as she calls him in her romantic daydreams. Vicki also has a passion for ballet—after six years of classes, she has been accepted into the demanding six-week summer program at New York's prestigious School of American Ballet. Vicki stays in the city with her mom's hip best friend, an aspiring actress. All this excitement doesn't allow Vicki to escape her anger and confusion over her parents' pending divorce, however. In just six weeks, Vicki learns more than she could have imagined—not just about dance, but also about herself and the wider world around her. And, to her surprise, a hard-working young man threatens to rival Misha in Vicki's daydreams. Martha Southgate's first novel, *Another Way to Dance* sweeps readers up in the excitement of dance—and a young woman discovering her own inner grace.

Grade 6 to Adult

Roll of Thunder, Hear My Cry

(1976)

Mildred D. Taylor. Frontispiece by Jerry Pinkney

276 pages

Set in Mississippi in 1933, *Roll of Thunder, Hear My Cry* is a breathtaking novel examining the cruelty of racism as seen from nine-year-old Cassie Logan's perspective. She and her brothers are raised with love and pride by their parents and grandmother. Unlike most of their share-cropping neighbors, the Logans own their land. But despite their relative good fortune, nothing can shield Cassie and her brothers from the violence erupting in their community. The trouble begins with a deadly attack on three African American men by the Wallaces, the town's white store-owners. When the attack goes unpunished, Cassie's parents organize a black boycott of the Wallace store—no easy feat, and a dangerous one at that. Things really explode when her older brother's friend, T. J. Avery, gets mixed up with some white teens. Readers will identify with Cassie's pain and bewilderment as some of her childhood innocence is stripped away by the events that unfold. This wonderful story—and all of Taylor's books about the Logan family— will captivate young and old alike.

Grade 6 to Adult

"*The thunder was creeping closer now, rolling angrily over the forest depths and bringing the lightning with it, as we emerged from the path into the deserted Avery yard.*"

Mildred Taylor
Roll of Thunder, Hear My Cry

I Hadn't Meant to Tell You This
(1994)
Jacqueline Woodson
115 pages

Nobody in Chauncey, Ohio, thinks it's wise for Marie and Lena to become friends. Segregation is the unwritten rule in the prosperous, mostly African American suburb, where the few white residents live in a run-down, poverty-stricken neighborhood. Eighth graders Marie and Lena break through these barriers to form a deep friendship; beneath their differences, they discover that they are soul mates. Marie lives in middle-class comfort, but grieves the absence of her mother, a depressed would-be artist who left Marie and her dad, and now occasionally sends mysterious postcards from cities around the world. Lena's mother, who couldn't afford medical care, died of breast cancer and Lena carries with her a heavy secret—the sexual abuse she, and now her eight-year-old sister, face at their father's hands. Lena confides in Marie, but swears her to secrecy, not trusting a social service system that once tried to separate her from her sister. Author Jacqueline Woodson treats these excruciating subjects with sensitivity and honesty in this absorbing novel.

Grade 6 to Adult

Gorilla, My Love
(1972)
Toni Cade Bambara
177 pages

This wonderful book offers readers the short story at its best. At once laugh-out-loud funny and dead serious, the stories in this collection command a reader's attention as if they were being told aloud. Toni Cade Bambara introduces readers to feisty, intelligent, streetwise voices who tell the stories of their lives. In "Gorilla, My Love," "Raymond's Run," and "Happy Birthday," Bambara brings the humor and searing injustice of childhood betrayals to the surface, always from a young girl's unique perspective. In other stories—"The Hammer Man," "The Lesson," and "Playin with Punjab"—poverty, racism, and police brutality are viewed through the eyes of girls who are hip to what's going on, but unable to fully comprehend the injustice they face. These well-crafted characters will stick with readers for some time to come. With *Gorilla, My Love*, Toni Cade Bambara earned her place as a master storyteller— one who brings the voice of young girls and women to the forefront of African American storytelling.

Grade 8 to Adult

Betsey Brown: A Novel
(1985)

Ntozake Shange

207 pages

At thirteen, Betsey Brown is caught somewhere between girl and woman—she's not ready to quit climbing into her favorite hiding spot in the "ancient" oak outside her bedroom window, but she's also eagerly awaiting the kisses of a certain basketball-playing Eugene Boyd. This charming novel takes readers to St. Louis in 1959, where Betsey lives in a well-to-do African American neighborhood with her parents, her very old-fashioned grandmother, two sisters, a brother, a cousin, and a never-ending stream of housekeeper/babysitters. Each morning, the Brown kids line up for their father's morning quiz, in which he asks them questions about black history and culture, adding an extra nickel to their lunch money if they answer correctly. In this bustling, almost chaotic household bursting with lively arguments, music, pride, and love, Betsey Brown struggles to define herself. Complicating these growing-up thoughts are serious issues like integration, civil rights, and questions of class. Well-written and full of zest, *Betsey Brown* is a novel to be savored.

Grade 8 to Adult

"*The uppermost branches stretched past her very own window, so Betsey knew this was her tree, where she could think all kinds of thoughts and feel all kinds of feelings.*"

Ntozake Shange
Betsey Brown

The Road to Memphis

(1990)

Mildred D. Taylor

290 pages

M ildred Taylor brilliantly paints Cassie Logan's hopes and dreams against a backdrop of the harsh realities of her life in 1941 Mississippi. Seventeen-year-old Cassie, her older brother Stacey, and their friends are changing a tire on Stacey's car when the worst possible thing happens: three young white men begin viciously taunting their friend, Moe. In an instant that would change their lives forever, Moe fights back rather than silently take the abuse as was expected, seriously injuring the men. For Moe to stay in the area would mean his death, so Cassie and Stacey know they must secretly drive him to safety. They embark on a painful, perilous adventure to Memphis, Tennessee, where Moe will be able to board a train for Chicago. *The Road to Memphis*, fast-paced and dramatic, is one of several wonderful novels that focus on the Logan family.

Grade 8 to Adult

Like Sisters on the Homefront
(1995)
Rita Williams-Garcia
165 pages

Defiant and stubborn, Gayle is a fourteen-year-old
mother and pregnant for the second time when this unique
novel opens. Concerned with little more than hanging on
to "her man," Gayle is upset when her mother forces her to
have an abortion. She's even angrier when her mother
sends Gayle and her baby down South to live with relatives
that the New York teen has never even met—her mother's
strict brother, who is a preacher, his wife, and their daughter.
Personalities immediately clash—Gayle can't believe the
innocence of her sixteen-year-old, kneesocks-wearing
cousin, Cookie. She doesn't see how she and her baby
will fit into this strict religious family at all until she meets
Great, her bed-ridden great-grandmother whose razor-
sharp tongue is a match for her own. Slowly, Gayle starts
to see herself and her future in a different light, as she
discovers that she and Cookie are "like sisters on the home-
front" despite all their differences.

Grade 8 to Adult

Kindred

(1979)

Octavia E. Butler

264 pages

Full of mystery, suspense, and adventure, *Kindred* will have readers racing to its conclusion. The year is 1976, and as twenty-six-year-old Dana unpacks her belongings in the California home she and her husband have just bought, a sudden wave of nausea and dizziness overtakes her. Inexplicably, she finds herself transported to another place and time. As these episodes recur, she learns that her destination is a Maryland plantation in the 1800s—populated with her ancestors, both slaves and masters. She's transported to this setting by her white great-grandfather, Rufus Weylin, whenever his life is in danger, starting when he is five years old and continuing periodically until his death. In turn, Dana can only return to her own place and time when she believes *her* life is in danger. Viewing slavery from the perspective of a contemporary woman, *Kindred* is a fascinating novel that will leave a deep imprint on readers.

Grade 10 to Adult

A Piece of Mine
(1984)
J. California Cooper
124 pages

The art of storytelling infuses these flavorful tales with energy and zest. Each of the short stories in *A Piece of Mine* is written as if the narrator is speaking aloud, often in the familiar style one might use to swap anecdotes with a good friend. "$100 and Nothing!" opens the book, introducing readers to Mary, a sweet, hard-working woman who marries a no-good man who treats her so horribly that she dies of a broken heart. Told from the perspective of Mary's best friend, the story explains how Mary gets her revenge on this evil man from beyond the grave, because, as the narrator explains, "we hoe our own rows and what we plants there, we picks." On the other hand, virtue is rewarded in "Funeral Plans." A kind woman has spent her youth dutifully caring for crippled parents; now she's in her forties, her folks have passed away, and she's hatched a plan to find a husband to love. J. California Cooper gives an unusual twist to age-old tales of virtue, innocence, and guilt in this lively book.

Grade 10 to Adult

Krik? Krak!

(1995)

Edwidge Danticat

224 pages

The intense and often silent bond between mothers and daughters is captured in this stunning collection of nine short stories by Edwidge Danticat, who was in her mid-twenties when this book was published. Danticat's words are as beautiful as the landscape of paradise, while the stories they tell are tragedies stemming from violent political oppression in her homeland of Haiti. In "Children of the Sea" a young girl in Haiti and her fleeing lover at sea keep a promise to write letters to each other though their messages can never be sent; in "Between the Pool and the Gardenias" a woman who is unable to bear a child finds an abandoned baby girl whom she imagines was meant just for her; in "The Missing Peace" a woman comes to Haiti from America in search of the remains of her mother, and is guided to a forbidden graveyard by a sixteen-year-old Haitian girl whose own mother died at her birth. Heavy with both love and anguish, these astonishing stories show the powerful nature of women facing the most horrible atrocities.

Grade 10 to Adult

The Best Short Stories by Negro Writers: An Anthology from 1899 to the Present

(1967)
Edited and with an introduction by Langston Hughes
508 pages

Edited by Langston Hughes, this anthology showcases the talents of nearly fifty outstanding writers. Encountering works from Richard Wright and Ralph Ellison to Alice Childress, Dorothy West, and other less-known authors, readers will take a journey through African American literary history. Charles Chesnutt writes about a white sheriff's unexpected encounter with his African American son; Zora Neale Hurston tells us about the playful love between a woman and her husband; and Alice Walker describes a girl's special relationship with the elderly, if not always sober, Mr. Sweet, a kindly guitar-playing neighbor. All of these stories offer glimpses into the great talents of their authors. When it was published in 1967, Hughes billed the book as the most comprehensive collection of African American short stories in existence, and it remains an impressive treasure of literary achievement today.

Grade 10 to Adult

Their Eyes Were Watching God
(1937)

Zora Neale Hurston

286 pages

When Janie Crawford is sixteen years old, she stretches out under a pear tree, dreamily contemplating the forces of nature, and has a revelation: "She had glossy leaves and bursting buds and she wanted to struggle with life but it seemed to elude her." From this point on, Janie embarks on a search for the love that will make her bloom. It leads her to two unhappy marriages and many hardships before she finally finds the love she has been waiting for all her life. When *Their Eyes Were Watching God* was first published in 1937, African American male critics, including Richard Wright, harshly criticized author Zora Neale Hurston. The focus of this novel—the coming of age of a sensitive young woman—did not mesh with her critics' political sensibilities. Today, the book is recognized as a classic. A poignant, beautiful novel that surges with passion, *Their Eyes Were Watching God* will captivate young women with its language and its wisdom.

Grade 10 to Adult

The Autobiography of My Mother
(1996)
Jamaica Kincaid
228 pages

N*o love: I could live in a place like this.*" The calm and steady voice of a motherless girl telling the unfolding story of her own passage to womanhood creates the mood of this extraordinary novel. She is so intensely alone, and such a keen observer of her development, that she remembers details of her own experience with the clarity of an outsider; yet her feelings remain so sharp that what would seem tragedy to the average person becomes an affirmation of life. Set in a sparsely populated island of the Caribbean, with vivid descriptions of nature and seemingly commonplace occurrences, this novel describes life in the care—or neglect—of the various homes in which the girl lives after her mother dies in childbirth. With this story, Jamaica Kincaid has created a masterpiece, showing the uncommon strength that comes with raising oneself in the absence of love.

Grade 10 to Adult

The Sleeper Wakes: Harlem Renaissance Stories by Women

(1993)

Edited and with an introduction by Marcy Knopf.
Foreword by Nellie Y. McKay
277 pages

ditor Marcy Knopf unearths nearly forgotten literary
gems in this lively collection of short stories. Women were
a very significant part of the Harlem Renaissance of the
1920s, but all too often their accomplishments have been
overlooked in favor of the male artists of the period. *The
Sleeper Wakes* intends to help remedy this imbalance. While
some of the women in this anthology are already well
known—Nella Larsen, Dorothy West, Zora Neale
Hurston—the writings of many others, like Gwendolyn
Bennett, Marita Bonner, Georgia Douglas Johnson, and
Anita Scott Coleman, cannot be easily found in print. For
many of the stories this book is indeed an awakening; it
marks the first time they have appeared in the public eye
since their original publication in such popular magazines
of the Harlem Renaissance as *The Crisis* and *Opportunity*.
This book at once entertains and reminds us of how great
talents can go unrecognized in the glare of others' glory.

Grade 10 to Adult

Passing
(1929)
Nella Larsen
215 pages

S et in 1927 Harlem, *Passing* reunites two childhood friends, both women with skin light enough to pass for white. Irene, a mother of two and the wife of a prominent doctor, lives in the world of black upper-class society. Clare passes in the white world, having married and had a child with an avowedly racist man who knows nothing of her secret. After years without contact, a chance meeting sparks an intense desire on Clare's part to become part of Irene's life—and social world. Though Irene voices disapproval of Clare's choices, she finds herself unable to say no to her old friend; the two are bound by a connection for which they have no name. Told from Irene's point of view, *Passing* will hold readers spellbound with its dramatic story of conflicts provoked by uneasily renewed friendship. An important novel of the Harlem Renaissance, *Passing* is brilliant testimony to Nella Larsen's talent.

Grade 10 to Adult

Brown Girl, Brownstones

(1959)

Paule Marshall

310 pages

The rebellious spirit of a young woman struggling to define herself in 1940s Brooklyn pervades this classic novel. When readers first meet Selina Boyce, she is ten years old. The tension between her parents, immigrants from Barbados, is swirling around her. Selina is torn between them; she's very close to her father, a mellow, loving man who dreams of returning to Barbados. Yet she's painfully aware of his flaws, including laziness and infidelity. Selina's mother is strong-willed, ambitious, and hard-working, but she is so unyielding in her pursuit of upward mobility that she can be rigid and cruel. She often clashes with her strong-willed daughter. Throughout the book, Selina refuses to fill the roles that others have chosen for her. By the age of seventeen, she has consciously rejected the coping strategies of those around her—and become more determined than ever to follow her own path, wherever it may lead. Beautifully written, *Brown Girl, Brownstones* is a poetic coming-of-age story introducing readers to the magic of Paule Marshall.

Grade 10 to Adult

Tempest Rising: A Novel
(1998)

Diane McKinney-Whetstone

280 pages

A s *Tempest Rising* opens, Clarise lives a charmed life in Philadelphia with her adoring husband Finch, who owns a successful catering business, and their three daughters: thirteen-year-old Shern, twelve-year-old Victoria, and eleven-year-old Bliss. Then tragedy strikes when Finch is caught out at sea and drowns. Just a month later, Clarise attempts suicide, her mind clouded by the strong drug her doctor has prescribed for her nerves. Before their aunts and uncles are able to take them in, the girls are immediately placed in foster care on the working-class side of town, in the house of a gambling woman and her beautiful but mean-spirited daughter Ramona. Ripped from everything they know, Shern, Victoria, and Bliss pull together for support, but discover their own individual strength as well. This gripping novel, with its dramatic conclusion, offers a wonderful message of redemption and strength.

Grade 10 to Adult

Disappearing Acts

(1989)

Terry McMillan

384 pages

Zora Banks and Franklin Swift are each taking a break from the opposite sex when they meet in a Brooklyn brownstone. Zora, almost thirty, a music teacher, singer, and songwriter with a fancy for food and tall men, is staying single because she's sick of being hurt and wants to focus on her singing. Franklin, in his early thirties, a tall, gifted woodworker sporadically employed in construction jobs, is trying to get his life together, and women complicate his plans. Set in 1982, the story is told in alternating chapters from Zora's and Franklin's sometimes very different points of view. At first, their relationship is perfect: they talk about their dreams, play Scrabble, debate politics, and spend a great deal of time in the bedroom. But as time goes by, all-too-common troubles arise. Neither Franklin nor Zora is completely honest with the other, causing problems that threaten to destroy their relationship. Peppered with sexual innuendo and explicit love scenes, *Disappearing Acts* will leave readers desperate to discover whether Zora and Franklin's love will triumph.

Grade 10 to Adult

Beloved
(1987)
Toni Morrison
275 pages

B*eloved* weaves together the gut-wrenching stories of women and men recovering from their painful journeys from slavery to freedom. At the center of the book is Sethe, who was not yet twenty years old, pregnant, and already the mother of three the night she made her escape from the plantation known in happier times as "Sweet Home." She nearly dies trying to find her way North, giving birth along the way. The events surrounding her desperate escape set in motion a chain of monstrosities that continues to affect her life nearly twenty years later, in 1873. As the novel opens, Sethe has deadened herself to the past, shutting down her emotions in order to bear her life, but a series of events forces her to break open old wounds in order to heal. Amazingly complex and haunting, *Beloved* is an American masterpiece and the novel that helped earn its author the 1993 Nobel Prize in literature.

Grade 10 to Adult

The Bluest Eye

(1970)

Toni Morrison

164 pages

B orn into a family battered and withered by years of hatred, poverty, and unhappiness, eleven-year-old Pecola Breedlove prays every night for one simple wish: to have blue eyes. Pecola believes that to have blue eyes would be to have the beauty that she, and everyone around her, sees in white girls. If she had blue eyes, Pecola reasons, her father would no longer drink, her mother would no longer beat her, and she would no longer be an outcast. Most of all, everyone would stop blaming her for her own suffering. Pecola's story is told largely from the perspective of Claudia, a classmate. She and her sister are the only people who can see Pecola's worth. After Pecola's drunken father impregnates her, they are the only ones to feel sorrow for her. Yet this novel also incorporates the stories of Pecola's parents and other adults in her life, offering complicated insight into their cruel behavior. Toni Morrison's first novel, *The Bluest Eye* is a masterful declaration of the value and beauty of African American girls, and a stinging indictment of a society that often refuses to see it.

Grade 10 to Adult

Mama Day
(1988)

Gloria Naylor

312 pages

B ring your troubles to Mama Day and, if she can, she'll take nature's gifts and create a remedy for your complaints. But when Mama Day's young niece, Cocoa, brings her husband home for the first time to meet her and Cocoa's grandmother, Mama Day's remedies are put to the test as never before. The setting of the story moves between the concrete and steel of New York, where Cocoa and her husband live and work, and the lush, beautiful, and stateless island where Cocoa grew up and where Mama Day still lives. On this island, some can still feel the odd stirrings of an ancestor of nearly two centuries ago who started the line that has brought us to Cocoa's generation. Tragedy hovers at the edge of the isolated island, especially when a tremendous storm hits and destroys the only bridge connecting it to the mainland. Conjuring the fierce, untameable powers of nature and blood, Gloria Naylor has created a passionate, haunting tale of love.

Grade 10 to Adult

The Street

(1946)
Ann Petry
435 pages

T*he thing that really mattered was getting away from Pop
and his raddled women, and anything was better than that. Dark
hallways, dirty stairs, even roaches on the wall. Anything.*" These
are the thoughts going through Lutie Johnson's head as
she looks for an apartment for herself and her eight-year-
old son, Bub, whom she's determined to wrench free of
her father's bad influence. A single mom in 1940s Harlem,
Lutie struggles to make ends meet. She's determined to
find a way out of the poverty, danger, and worst of all, the
hopelessness that haunts her neighborhood. But author
Ann Petry shows that despite her greatest intentions, the
forces steering Lutie's fate have her blindly set on a course
of destruction. A masterpiece of American literature, *The
Street* makes a fierce statement about the vicious cycle of
racism and poverty that remains chillingly relevant today,
over fifty years since its publication.

Grade 10 to Adult

"*And Lutie thought, No one could live on a street like this and stay decent. It would get them sooner or later, for it sucked the humanity out of people—slowly, surely, inevitably.*"

Ann Petry
The Street

Clover: A Novel

(1990)
Dori Sanders
183 pages

This unique novel is told in the voice of ten-year-old Clover Hill. Set in 1980s South Carolina, it opens just after her father's marriage to a white woman named Sara Kate, against everyone's wishes. Clover's dad, whom she calls Gaten, dies in a car accident hours after the wedding. In the wake of this tragedy, to everyone's surprise and displeasure, Sara Kate announces that she promised Gaten she'd take care of his daughter. Because "nobody around here messes with a dying man's wishes," the matter is settled—Clover will live with her new stepmother. While Clover is slow to warm up to Sara Kate, her Aunt Everleen and Uncle Jim Ed are even more distrustful. The colorful community of Round Hill, home of the Hill peach farm, forms a vibrant backdrop to Clover's sharp observations as she—and everyone around her—tries to find their way in uncharted territory. Spirited, smart, and amusing, Clover's surprisingly wise voice will delight readers.

Grade 10 to Adult

The Good Negress
(1995)
A. J. Verdelle
298 pages

Denise—called Neesey—is seven years old when her father dies suddenly on Easter Sunday. Soon after, her mother brings her down South to temporarily live with her Gran'maam, who comforts the grieving girl with this advice: "The best way to make y'self feel better is to get y'hands to workin." Five years later, Neesey is called back "home" to Detroit to help out now that her remarried mother is pregnant. She heeds Gran'maam's advice, cleaning everything in sight, taking over the kitchen, and studying every free minute. For Neesey, learning is an escape from the uncertain ground of her family life, but her mother views her as the nursemaid to her baby sister. Neesey forms special bonds with her teacher, who tutors her in "proper" English and so much more, and with Josephus, a special friend who gives Neesey the love and support she's missing at home. First-time novelist A. J. Verdelle has crafted a brilliant window into the innermost thoughts of a young woman who slowly recognizes that language will give her the power to shape her own future.

Grade 10 to Adult

The Color Purple
(1982)
Alice Walker
245 pages

I n this classic, Pulitzer Prize–winning novel, Alice
Walker explores the incredible healing journey of a young
woman left scarred and numbed by cruelty and abuse. As
The Color Purple opens, writing letters to God is Celie's
single, silent act of protest against the torment she endures.
The novel takes the form of Celie's letters, written as if she
were telling her troubles to a close friend. By the age of
twenty, Celie, forced into an abusive, loveless marriage, has
already given up any hope of changing her life. As she says,
"I don't fight, I stay where I'm told. But I'm alive." Her
bleak outlook slowly changes when her husband's blues-
singer mistress, Shug Avery, comes into their home. Shug
awakens both Celie's sexuality and a realization of her own
self-worth. Readers will eagerly devour Celie's letters, first
to God, later to her long-lost sister, as they chart her
progress through anger and forgiveness and finally to love
and happiness. With *The Color Purple*, Alice Walker has
created a masterpiece of American literature. A must read.

Grade 10 to Adult

Jubilee
(1966)
Margaret Walker
497 pages

I n this long, dramatic, easy-to-read novel, Margaret Walker has lovingly crafted a story inspired by the remarkable life of her great-grandmother, Elvira Ware Dozier, known to her loved ones as Vyry. She was born into slavery, of a father who was also her master, and for this fact she suffers greatly at the hands of her jealous mistress, Big Missy, as she works in the big house, first as a maid for her half-sister Lillian, and later as a cook. During this time, Vyry falls in love with a free man, marries him, and has two children by him. *Jubilee* takes readers from her failed attempts to gain freedom for herself and her children, to the turbulent years of the Civil War, when her husband leaves to fight in the Union army, to the bewildering first days after emancipation, the search for land, and the struggle to provide an education for her children. Despite all the obstacles placed in her path, Vyry refuses to sacrifice her morals or her dignity. Readers will be left spellbound by this romantic, sweeping look at the life of a brave woman.

Grade 10 to Adult

Devil's Gonna Get Him

(1995)

Valerie Wilson Wesley

212 pages

In her second Tamara Hayle mystery, Valerie Wilson Wesley has created a fast-paced and entertaining story that keeps the reader guessing to the end. Hayle, a private investigator and former policewoman, steps into sticky business when she agrees to work for Lincoln Storey, a very wealthy and offensive man who is searching for information about his daughter's lover. Storey is dead within hours of their conversation—poisoned by peanut butter—and the police pin the murder on the daughter of Hayle's good friend. Hayle sets out to discover who truly committed the murder, but it seems that everyone surrounding Storey— relatives, lovers, and business acquaintances—had a motive to do away with him. Readers will be riveted as the down-to-earth, crafty Hayle sifts through the evidence, while revisiting some painful memories from her own past, to solve the case.

Grade 10 to Adult

Soul Kiss

(1997)
Shay Youngblood
207 pages

T he beautifully poetic and heartrending tone of this book is felt at the outset. "The first evening Mama doesn't come back, I make a sandwich with leaves from her good-bye letter. I want to eat her words." One day without warning, seven-year-old Mariah's mother mysteriously brings her on a train from Kansas to Georgia and leaves her with two great-aunts in a picture-perfect old house. The story of Mariah's unending wait for her mother to return to her, as she becomes a teenager and then a young college student, is as seamless as if time stood still. Yet much happens as Mariah's sensuality blossoms, and she begins to unravel the complex threads of her identity, meeting her artist father, Matisse, for the first time, and experimenting with love. At once explicit and poetic, *Soul Kiss* grips the reader with its quiet force, and leaves an impression on the mind as if a secret message has been left there, waiting to reveal itself.

Grade 10 to Adult

Autobiographies
and
Biographies

Wilma Unlimited: How Wilma Rudolph Became the World's Fastest Woman

(1996)

Kathleen Krull. Illustrations by David Diaz
Unpaged

W hen Wilma Rudolph was born in Clarksville, Tennessee, in 1940, her parents and nineteen brothers and sisters worried about her health because she was so tiny and sickly. Between illnesses, Wilma was extremely active, always running and jumping. But when she was almost five years old, Wilma caught polio and it seemed as though she'd never walk again without a sturdy metal brace. No one could imagine what she would achieve fifteen years later: earning three gold medals in track and field for the United States in the 1960 Olympic Games, thus proving herself the world's fastest woman. *Wilma Unlimited* tells the fascinating and inspirational story of how Wilma overcame every barrier in her path with hard work and tireless spirit. Brilliant full-page illustrations convey this woman's strength and energy, and make the book a winning tribute to her.

Picture Book to Adult

Going Back Home: An Artist Returns to the South

(1996)

Paintings by Michele Wood. Story interpreted and written by Toyomi Igus

Unpaged

As a girl growing up in Indiana, artist Michele Wood loved to listen to stories about her family's Southern heritage. This interest stayed with her into adulthood, leading her to research the history of her family. In this book, readers will find the fruit of her work: a stunning series of richly colored, quilt-like paintings she created to reflect the experiences of her ancestors. The artist's own explanation of the paintings has been written with young readers in mind. *Going Back Home* transports readers to the struggles of slavery, the enduring strength of the family, the unfair system of sharecropping, and more. Although Wood is imagining the experiences of her own ancestors, *Going Back Home* prompts young readers to consider a rich history that belongs to them and to all African Americans.

Picture Book to Adult

May Chinn: The Best Medicine
(1995)

Ellen R. Butts and Joyce R. Schwartz. Illustrations by
Janet Hamlin
48 pages

orn in 1896, May Chinn succeeded against all odds
to become one of the first African American women
doctors in Harlem. Throughout May's childhood, her
mother did everything possible to see that she got the
best education. May attended college in Harlem as the
Harlem Renaissance began to unfold around her. After
graduating, she became a doctor at a time when this
nation had virtually no African American women doctors.
May started her own medical practice in Harlem, and
treated many people who might otherwise have gone
without medical care, especially women and children. As a
doctor, May fought fiercely against discrimination, helping
to bring about important changes to ensure medical care
for those with little means. With respect and admiration,
this biography shines a deserving light on May Chinn's
often overlooked achievements.

Grades 4 to 7

What I Had Was Singing:
The Story of Marian Anderson
(1994)
Jeri Ferris
96 pages; illustrations

As a child in South Philadelphia just after the turn
of the century, Marian Anderson loved to sing. By the time
she was in high school, she was singing in front of audiences
nearly every day, most often at black churches and colleges.
Her voice amazed everyone who heard it, but even so,
young Marian needed training and practice to make the
most of her talent. Years of hard work paid off: by the late
1930s, Anderson was an acclaimed singer in the United
States and Europe. On Easter Sunday in 1939, after she
had been barred from singing at Constitution Hall because
of her color, she performed at the Lincoln Memorial in
Washington, D.C., for an audience of over 75,000. In
1955, she became the first African American to sing with
the Metropolitan Opera in New York—a childhood dream
come true. A delight to read and page through, with its
fabulous black-and-white photographs, *What I Had Was
Singing* is a rich portrait of an American heroine.

Grades 4 to 7

She Dared to Fly: Bessie Coleman
(1997)

Dolores Johnson

48 pages; illustrations

F ree-wheeling and adventurous, Bessie Coleman made history in 1921 when she became the first African American to receive a pilot's license. When Bessie's brother returned home from World War I, he delighted in teasing his spirited younger sister about the independence of French women; some of them, he said, even flew airplanes. In that instant, Bessie decided that she, too, would become a pilot. The only problem: American flight schools refused to enroll women or African American students. Undaunted, Bessie saved her money and sailed to France to take flying lessons. Back home, she began the near-impossible search for a pilot's job; in many parts of the country, her race and sex prevented her from even buying a plane. Nonetheless, Bessie became a talented stunt pilot at airshows, and worked toward her dream of founding a flying school that would be open to both men and women, and all races. This thoughtful biography, sprinkled with charming photos, celebrates the joyful courage of a woman who broke down barrier after barrier.

Grades 4 to 7

"It is because Bessie Coleman dared to fly that countless people—black and white, young and old, women and men—can dare to dream their dreams and achieve them."

Dolores Johnson
She Dared to Fly: Bessie Coleman

Mary McLeod Bethune
(1992)

Patricia C. and Fredrick McKissack
30 pages; illustrations

When she was a small child, Mary Jane McLeod's greatest dream was to learn how to read. She was born in 1875, and was the first of her parents' fifteen children to be born into freedom. It was a very difficult time for African American children to get an education, so when a church set up a school in her town of Mayesville, South Carolina, young Mary Jane was elated. When she grew up, Mary McLeod Bethune started her own school for young African American girls in Daytona, Florida. Bethune had very little money with which to support this ever-growing school—in its early years, her students substituted boxes for desks—but her enthusiasm and passion for learning convinced many, including some of the country's wealthiest businessmen, to contribute to the cause. Today her school, known as Bethune-Cookman College, educates thousands of young women and men each year. Full of interesting photographs, this biography highlights Bethune's achievements with pride.

Grades 4 to 9

Charlotte Forten: A Black Teacher in the Civil War

(1995)
Peter Burchard
106 pages; illustrations

This fascinating biography draws on Charlotte Forten's diaries, which she started keeping at the age of sixteen. Born into a highly educated free family in Philadelphia in 1837, Charlotte Forten grew up surrounded by talented women and men who would leave their own marks on history as crusaders against slavery, and who are also described in detail in this book. Charlotte was a young school teacher of twenty-five when the Civil War broke out and during the war she volunteered to teach the children of escaped slaves. On what she described as "the most glorious day this nation has yet seen" she celebrated the Emancipation Proclamation of January 1, 1863, with other abolitionists, freed slaves, and black Union soldiers. The unique life of Charlotte Forten will charm readers of this first-rate biography for young people.

Grade 6 to Adult

Big Star Fallin' Mama:
Five Women in Black Music

(1995)
Hettie Jones
150 pages; illustrations

C harming and intelligent, this book celebrates the music and lives of five women who have made astronomical contributions to American music. Author Hettie Jones opens her book with Ma Rainey, the first of the great blues singers, who traveled the United States singing the country blues of the South. She helped lay the groundwork for Bessie Smith, who became known as the Empress of Blues and recorded many songs in the 1920s. Readers will also meet Mahalia Jackson, who became a world-famous gospel singer; Billie Holiday, a brilliant jazz singer who used her voice like an instrument; and Aretha Franklin, who is still singing today. Drawing upon photographs, quotes from other musicians, and lyrics, Jones brings to life the world surrounding these stars. A new edition of a book first published in 1974, *Big Star Fallin' Mama* invites readers to immerse themselves in the music of legendary women.

Grade 6 to Adult

Sojourner Truth: Ain't I a Woman?
(1992)

Patricia C. and Fredrick McKissack

186 pages; illustrations

R evered as an abolitionist, women's rights activist, and persuasive public speaker, Sojourner Truth was a woman who attracted attention—and demanded respect. In their detailed biography the McKissacks celebrate the life of this woman, who was born in New York in 1797. Given the slave name Isabella, she renamed herself Sojourner Truth after she was freed as an adult, as a symbol of her deep religious faith. From that day forward, Sojourner began a new life of travel and lecturing. The book's title comes from a famous speech in which Sojourner refuted hostile arguments that women were inferior to men by pointing out the things she'd done in her life, repeating after each: "And ain't I a woman?" This biography for young people places the life of Sojourner Truth in a rich historical context, and is supplemented by many illustrations and photographs. Courageous, wise, and respected in her own lifetime, Sojourner Truth remains a legend today.

Grade 6 to Adult

Rosa Parks: My Story
(1992)

Rosa Parks and James Haskins

192 pages; illustrations

osa Parks catapulted into the history books when she sparked the famous Montgomery, Alabama, bus boycott in December 1955 by refusing to give up her seat to a white man on a segregated bus. Her moving autobiography gives readers a chance to read about this historic event from Rosa Parks's own point of view. Though many accounts have downplayed her activism by describing her as a tired seamstress, as she describes it here, "The only tired I was, was tired of giving in." Parks fills readers in on her childhood, when she became aware of the ravages of racism at a very young age; her young adult years, when she became an activist with the NAACP; the boycott itself; and beyond, to her lifelong crusade for human rights. This fascinating autobiography, written in a friendly, conversational tone, will give readers a well-rounded portrait of the woman who came to symbolize the fight for civil rights.

Grade 6 to Adult

Harriet Tubman: Conductor on the Underground Railroad
(1955)
Ann Petry
247 pages

W hen Harriet Tubman was a young girl living on Maryland's Eastern Shore, she heard whispers floating through the slave quarters about something called the Underground Railroad, which mysteriously transported slaves to freedom. Little did she imagine that one day she would be the most famous conductor on the Underground Railroad, which was actually a code word for the secret system of people who risked their lives to help slaves escape. This biography will thrill readers with its descriptions of Harriet's own daring escape (against her husband's wishes) and her more than fifteen trips back into slave territory to rescue hundreds of others. In all these trips, the fearless Harriet Tubman never lost a single "passenger." After each chapter, acclaimed author Ann Petry fills readers in on other historical events related to the anti-slavery movement. This fascinating book reveals the real person behind the legend as it introduces readers to one of America's greatest heroines.

Grade 6 to Adult

Marian Wright Edelman: The Making of a Crusader

(1995)

Beatrice Siegel

159 pages; illustrations

R ich in historical detail, this biography shines a glowing light on Marian Wright Edelman and her work on behalf of America's children. Born in 1939, Marian Wright was the youngest of five children in a family that stressed the importance of education, hard work, and service to the community. Her upbringing in Bennettsville, South Carolina, within a strong African American community, provided the values that she would bring to her life's work. After graduating from Yale Law School, she moved to Mississippi and became the first African American woman admitted to the state's bar—thus placing herself on the frontlines of the civil rights protests. There, her efforts to secure federal support for the state's much needed Head Start program marked the beginning of her crusade for the well-being of all children in America. In the 1970s Marian Wright Edelman founded the Children's Defense Fund, a powerful organization that provokes the nation's conscience and pushes our leaders to care for all children.

Grade 6 to Adult

Mama's Girl

(1996)
Veronica Chambers
194 pages

As *double-dutch girls, we had our own prance."* Just in her twenties, accomplished journalist and author Veronica Chambers turns her pen to her own life in this wonderfully warm and inviting book. Eventually arriving at a plum job as an editor at the *New York Times*, Chambers tells a story that begins in a two-family apartment house in East Flatbush, with parents of Caribbean birth—an abusive father and a distant, though well-meaning mother whom she loves dearly. Despite these circumstances, Chambers blossoms at school. Along with her own good fortune, she tells the story of her younger brother who, though just as bright and energetic, takes turns that bring him into the grip of the law. With not a trace of bitterness, Chambers conveys the uplifting story of a young woman guiding her own destiny.

Grade 8 to Adult

In My Place

(1992)

Charlayne Hunter-Gault

257 pages; illustrations

I n this winning autobiography, Charlayne Hunter-Gault, long experienced in public broadcasting, turns a journalist's eye to her own coming of age. Hunter-Gault describes a childhood spent in the warm atmosphere created by her mother and grandmother. Inspired by the comic-strip adventures of Brenda Starr, young Charlayne decided she wanted to be a journalist. Journalism was offered in Georgia's white colleges only, so Charlayne initially attended a small school in Detroit. But, armed with the emotional and legal support of African American leaders, Charlayne and another bright Atlanta student, Hamilton Holmes, integrated the University of Georgia in 1961. Hunter-Gault writes about the violence and isolation she faced, as well as the opportunities, including a chance to write about her experiences for a variety of publications while she was in college. Sharp, witty, and well-documented, *In My Place* urges readers to shoot for their own dreams.

Grade 8 to Adult

Incidents in the Life of a Slave Girl, Written by Herself

(1861)

Harriet A. Jacobs. Edited by L. Maria Child

306 pages

This gripping autobiography tells of Harriet Jacobs's extraordinary struggle to become free in 1830s North Carolina. In the book, she describes the suffering she endured at the hands of a master who harassed her and constantly tried to make her his lover. One night, Jacobs could take no more and decided to run away. But before she could get out of town, her master had posted flyers with a reward for her capture and began conducting a massive search. Unwilling to return to him, and unable to leave, Jacobs took refuge in the only place possible: the crawl space in the house of her grandmother, who was a freed slave. Jacobs's apparently successful escape riled her obsessed master, who only beefed up his efforts to find the fugitive slave, forcing her to make the hiding space her home for seven long years. *Incidents in the Life of a Slave Girl* rings clear with the voice of an amazing woman.

Grade 8 to Adult

I Know Why the Caged Bird Sings

(1969)

Maya Angelou

281 pages

aking its title from a poem by Paul Laurence Dunbar, *I Know Why the Caged Bird Sings* is Maya Angelou's classic, razor-sharp chronicle of her girlhood. Extremely intelligent, shy, and awkward, young Maya idolized her older brother Bailey, with whom she shared her most private thoughts. At the age of three, Angelou and her brother lived in the strict but loving care of their grandmother in tiny, segregated Stamps, Arkansas. When her silver-tongued father showed up one day to bring them to live with their beautiful mother in St. Louis, Angelou says, "my seven-year-old world humpty-dumptied, never to be put back together again." There, Angelou faced severe trauma that caused her to stop speaking to everyone but Bailey. Angelou also takes readers through her adventurous teenage years when she lived with her mother in San Francisco during World War II. This riveting book describes with eloquence and pointed humor the pain of growing up African American and female, and will keep readers glued to the page.

Grade 10 to Adult

"We were on top again. As always, again. We survived.
The depths had been icy and dark, but now a bright
sun spoke to our souls."

Maya Angelou
I Know Why the Caged Bird Sings

Black Ice

(1991)

Lorene Cary

237 pages

I n 1972, Lorene Cary was one of the first women *and* African Americans to attend prestigious St. Paul's School in New Hampshire. For fifteen-year-old Lorene, leaving her family and Yeadon, their mostly black suburb of Philadelphia, seemed like an adventure. Ambitious and smart, she was eager to gain access to the elite education the school was offering her on a scholarship. With just a handful of African American classmates, however, Lorene found herself isolated and eternally questioning the affluence that most of the students took for granted. Distanced from her family and old friends, Lorene often felt as if "there was no solid ground" for her at St. Paul's, "but neither was there any going back." With the support of other black students, Lorene settled into the academically rigorous school, awakening the confidence and leadership within herself. Years later, Cary continued to wrestle with mixed emotions as a teacher at the school and later, a trustee. Cary brings these complicated feelings to light with easy grace in this frank, thought-provoking memoir.

Grade 10 to Adult

The Black Notebooks: An Interior Journey
(1997)
Toi Derricotte
205 pages

Deeply personal and elegantly written, *The Black Notebooks* explores issues of color and race as seen through the eyes of poet Toi Derricotte. Light-skinned, with so-called "good" hair and features, Derricotte often involuntarily passes into the white world. In this book she delves into her painful mixed feelings of her seeming double identity. She writes of her emotional paralysis whenever she's confronted with a white person's racism, and the internal dilemma she faces in reacting to the situation. Derricotte shares her complicated feelings, even when she's ashamed of them, bringing an astonishing level of introspective honesty to this book. One woman's passionate struggle to come to terms with the insanities of color and race in this country, *The Black Notebooks* will captivate dedicated readers.

Grade 10 to Adult

To Be Young, Gifted and Black: Lorraine Hansberry in Her Own Words

(1969)

Lorraine Hansberry. Adapted by Robert Nemiroff.
Introduction by James Baldwin
266 pages; illustrations

To Be Young, Gifted and Black stretches the boundaries of autobiography and drama to create a unique, collage-like portrait of playwright Lorraine Hansberry, who died of cancer at the age of 34, cutting short a brilliant career. By turns humorous, defiant, and personal, the writing in this unusual book has also been performed as a play. Compiled by Hansberry's ex-husband after her death, the book contains sections of her acclaimed *Raisin in the Sun* and other plays, along with previously unpublished letters, drawings, speeches, and diary entries. A wonderfully intimate introduction by James Baldwin offers a distinguished perspective on Hansberry's life and achievements. *To Be Young, Gifted, and Black* offers a rare glimpse into the heart and mind of a young genius.

Grade 10 to Adult

The Memphis Diary of Ida B. Wells: An Intimate Portrait of the Activist as a Young Woman
(1995)

Ida B. Wells. Edited and with an introduction by Miriam DeCosta-Willis. Foreword by Mary Helen Washington. Afterword by Dorothy Sterling
214 pages; illustrations

Ida B. Wells spearheaded a national crusade against lynching through her leadership and career as a journalist. This diary offers readers a revealing glimpse at her life as an ambitious young woman on the cusp of great accomplishment. Wells began keeping a diary in 1885, when she was twenty-four years old. Teaching in Memphis at the time, she writes about everyday concerns like finances, courtship, and housing, as well as her intense desire to better herself; she reads newspapers constantly, and writes up to seven letters a day, many to journalists. During the two years in which she kept this diary, she also published her first articles, a sampling of which are included here. Editor Miriam Decosta-Willis brings to light a wealth of information in this fascinating, well-researched book.

Grade 10 to Adult

Poetry

The Genie in the Jar
(1996)

Nikki Giovanni. Illustrations by Chris Raschka

Unpaged

Irresistibly charming, *The Genie in the Jar* introduces young people to the poetry of Nikki Giovanni. The book consists of a poem originally dedicated to singer Nina Simone, carrying its message to a younger audience here. As the poem opens, Giovanni invites readers to "take a note / and spin it around / spin it around." Just a few words appear on each page of this picture book, accentuating the rhythmic effects of the poem's repetition. Chris Raschka's brilliant illustrations of a young girl dancing and playing with her mother and others bring the poem to life. Adding to their childlike charm, the illustrations look as if they'd been drawn and painted on a brown paper bag. Readers of all ages will find themselves touched by the warmth and energy that pours from this book.

Picture Book to Grade 5

Under the Sunday Tree: Poems
(1988)

Eloise Greenfield. Illustrations by Amos Ferguson
38 pages

L̲ight-hearted and fun to read aloud, *Under the Sunday Tree* stresses the beauty of nature, the joy of animals, and the importance of family. Many of its poems are whimsical, like the rhyming "To Catch a Fish," which warns young people that to do so, "it takes more than a wish." In "Donkey," children sit on a donkey who refuses to move: "he's just going to stand right there / he says as much in donkey talk / 'Hee-haw, when you get down, I'll walk.'" These poems by Eloise Greenfield focus on life in the Bahamas, especially "Tradition" and "When the Tourists Come to Town," and Amos Ferguson's rich, boldly colored illustrations are based on his own childhood there. *Under the Sunday Tree* swells with energy—making the book a perfect choice to share with a young person.

Picture Book to Grade 5

Meet Danitra Brown

(1994)

Nikki Grimes. Illustrations by Floyd Cooper
Unpaged

anitra Brown is "the greatest, most splendiferous girl in town," as her best friend, Zuri Jackson, tells us in this collection of thirteen poems celebrating friendship. Young readers hear all about Danitra's quirks; she dresses entirely in purple because her mother told her it's the color queens wear in Timbuktu. Zuri also tells readers about Danitra's dreams, like winning the Nobel Prize someday. But most important to Zuri is what a good friend Danitra is: "Danitra knows just what to say to make me glad / with her around, I'm never lonely." Writing fresh, exuberant poetry from the perspective of a young girl, Nikki Grimes stresses the importance of remaining true to oneself and working toward dreams. Illustrator Floyd Cooper brings his usual magic to the full-color illustrations.

Picture Book, Grades 4 to 7

i live in music
(1994)

Ntozake Shange. Paintings/collages by Romare Bearden

Unpaged

This spellbinding picture book for all ages celebrates the wonder, pure joy, and magic of music. Ntozake Shange's poem "i live in music" teams up with the paintings and collages of Romare Bearden to create an explosion of color and rhythm. Although Shange and Bearden created these works separately, the art and poetry fit together as if each were created with the other in mind. The line "i live on c# avenue" is paired with a dramatic collage of a city scene. Shange is a musician, dancer, and actress, as well as a writer. Bearden was also a songwriter; he saw links between his artwork and the blues. *i live in music* promises to awaken young people to the genius of Ntozake Shange and Romare Bearden—and spark a new love of music, art, and poetry.

Picture Book to Adult

The Lost Zoo

(1940)

Countee Cullen and Christopher Cat

95 pages

Renowned Harlem Renaissance poet Countee Cullen cowrote this lively collection of poems with his persnickety feline companion, Christopher Cat. *The Lost Zoo* is a laugh-out-loud poetic retelling of the events surrounding Noah's Ark—especially the tales of those unlucky animals who missed the boat, like the Lapalakes and the Squilililigee. Christopher also introduces readers to the Twelve-Eyed Wakeupworld, the Sleepamitemore, and Hoodinkus-With-The-Double-Head. The Wakeupworld was too busy shooing every sleeping animal on its way; the other animals have equally ironic excuses. These tall tales were passed down, generation to generation, to Christopher Cat, a direct descendant of a cat who sailed on Noah's Ark. Full of rhymes and whimsical humor, all these poems are at their best when read aloud. Older readers in particular will appreciate Christopher's amusing poetic footnotes. Share this imaginative book with animal lovers of all ages.

Grade 4 to Adult

Honey, I Love and Other Love Poems
(1978)

Eloise Greenfield. Illustrations by Leo and Diane Dillon
Unpaged

Spirited and touching, *Honey, I Love* sparkles with the feelings and personality of a young girl. Readers will find simple, easy-to-read poems about the joys of jumping rope, listening to music, riding on a train, and other everyday activities side by side with more serious poems about the meaning of love and the value of a keepsake. Many celebrate the imagination, like "By Myself," in which a young girl closes her eyes and pretends she's all sorts of things, like "a squeaky noise," or "a leaf turning red," but when she opens her eyes, "What I care to be / Is me." The delightful illustrations evoke the mood of the 1970s, when this book was first published, as do a few references to seventies stars like the Jackson Five, but the feelings remain true today. Wonderful messages abound in this classic book of poetry for young readers.

Grade 4 to Adult

The Collected Poems of Langston Hughes
(1994)

Langston Hughes. Edited and with an introduction by
Arnold Rampersad
708 pages

A poetic treasure awaits readers who glimpse at the
pages of this hefty book showcasing decades of the poetry
that made Langston Hughes one of America's most
beloved writers. Hughes's poetry is arranged in roughly the
order in which it was written, taking readers on a journey
from his first poems as a teenager, including the now-classic
"The Negro Speaks of Rivers," to others that made him a
hero of the Harlem Renaissance, like "I, Too," up to the
experimental "Ask Your Mama." At the end of the book are
two special chapters, one containing poems published by
the Associated Negro Press, the other offering some of
Hughes's poetry written for young people. *The Collected
Poems of Langston Hughes* is a dynamic reflection of his
depth and versatility as a poet. A must read, whether for
the dedicated fan to pore over, front to back, or for new-
comers to flip through and become acquainted with the
genius of Langston Hughes.

Grade 4 to Adult

In the evening the city
Goes to bed
Hanging lights
About its head.

Langston Hughes
"City"
The Collected Poems of Langston Hughes

Mother Love: Poems

(1995)

Rita Dove

77 pages

Mother Love takes as its guiding theme the Greek myth
of Persephone and Demeter. In the ancient tale, young
Persephone is kidnapped by the god of the Underworld.
Her mother, Demeter, is so inconsolable with grief that she
refuses to tend to her duties as the goddess of agriculture,
allowing the earth to sink into the barren state of winter.
Rita Dove's brief foreword to this book fills readers in on
the background of the myth and shares the multilayered
meanings it holds for her as a daughter, mother, and poet.
The poems that follow—mostly sonnets—examine the myth
from all angles. In many, Dove specifically delves into the
myth, gracefully giving voice to Demeter's and Persephone's
different points of view. In others, Dove merely alludes to
the myth, discussing parallel issues today. Witty, invigorating,
and often surprising, *Mother Love* will be enjoyed by all.

Grade 8 to Adult

And Still I Rise

(1978)

Maya Angelou

54 pages

The beautifully crafted, elegant writing of Maya Angelou will captivate readers. This collection presents some of Angelou's now-classic poems, including the mesmerizing "Still I Rise," in which she boldly declares, "You may kill me with your hatefulness, / But still, like air, I'll rise." Many of these poems jump with the spirit of a party, like "Country Lover," a short rhyming poem that begins with the lines "Funky blues / Keen toed shoes." Several others swell with pride, including the notable "Phenomenal Woman." Other poems follow a more solemn track, like the stirring, personal "Kin." No matter what the mood, Angelou's poetry is smooth and honed to such utter perfection that reading it is an awe-inspiring experience. *And Still I Rise* showcases the talents of one of America's foremost poets. Savor this book.

Grade 10 to Adult

Selected Poems

(1963)

Gwendolyn Brooks

127 pages

I n 1950, Gwendolyn Brooks became the first African American to win a Pulitzer Prize. This collection draws on her first books of poetry: *A Street in Bronzeville*, the Pulitzer-winning *Annie Allen*, and *The Bean Eaters*, and also includes some previously unpublished poems. Readers will be charmed by the short rhyming poems like "We Real Cool" and "Sadie and Maud," which sound almost like nursery rhymes, but with a very serious twist. Equally delightful are the longer poems, like "The Sundays of Satin-Legs Smith," and the surprisingly tender "To Be in Love." Many of these poems claim the south side of Chicago as their setting, taking ordinary people and showing the magic of their lives. This collection of Gwendolyn Brooks's classic poems will delight everyone.

Grade 10 to Adult

The Book of Light: Poems
(1993)
Lucille Clifton
76 pages

T*he Book of Light* burns with quiet intensity. Lucille Clifton's poems explore the lingering memories of deep-seated pain with wit and forgiveness. They spring from sources extremely private, yet their pointed messages will speak to a wide audience. Many explore an abusive father, a man who has been battered by the circumstances of his own life: in "sam" Clifton asks, "oh stars / and stripes forever / what did you do to my father?" Clifton's sparse writing style accentuates the wry, understated humor that often forms a thin veil over the pain. One of several poems written to Superman, "final note to clark" shows a young girl chastising herself for "dreaming your x-ray vision / could see the beauty in me." Ultimately, this collection glows with hope: in a tribute to her great-grandmother, Clifton proclaims, "woman, i am / lucille, which stands for light," and so, too, do these radiant poems.

Grade 10 to Adult

We Are the Young Magicians
(1993)

Ruth Forman. Introduction by Cherríe Moraga
86 pages

In her first book of poetry, published at the age of twenty-four, Ruth Forman shakes up poetic conventions with no apologies. As a result, these poems jump off the page, as in "This Poem," which ends, "This poem slammin this poem black / n nobody tell me nothin cuz i said it / this poem be us n / this poem be poetry." Throughout *We Are the Young Magicians* Forman stresses that poetry is a tool for survival and, as such, it belongs to everyone. She stakes a claim on her power as a young black woman, bringing to her poetry subjects that have made an impact on her life, including the Gulf War, the beauty of black women, the warped realities of music videos, and the politics of class and education. Many of her poems race with urgency, as in her tribute to insomnia, a poem titled "3:59," which asks, "If everybody sleep / who be the one to call out in the black for justice?" Electrifying when read aloud, these poems offer an unspoken challenge to young women to put their own lives on paper—and to remain vigilant in the fight for equality.

Grade 10 to Adult

Coal
(1976)
Audre Lorde
70 pages

Audre Lorde's brilliant gifts are revealed in this collection of her early poems, some first published in 1968 when she was just in her thirties. As diamonds are pressed from coal, Lorde writes in the title poem, "I am Black because I come from the earth's inside / now take my word for jewel in the open night." In all of these poems, Lorde's writing is as finely etched as a cut gem, and the meanings of the words shift about, like light bouncing off the stone. She shares intimate truths of family, childbirth, and loss of love. Powerful visions of nature run through the poems, as in "Spring People": "At springtime and evening / I recall how we came / like new thunder / beating the earth / leaving the taste of rain and sunset / all our hungers before us." A great poet taken by illness too early in life, Audre Lorde left a legacy to be cherished in this moving collection of poems.

Grade 10 to Adult

Read with the Children

Storytelling is one of the great traditions of African American culture. Today, our authors tell stories, and all of us join in the tradition when we read and talk about books with each other and with our children. And just as Tom Feelings's *Middle Passage*—a story told in pictures—is a continuation of this practice, we hope *Strong Souls Singing* will also take its place in upholding this great tradition.

The custom of storytelling has endured because of its force: there is no better way to teach than to engage the imagination. Anyone who has ever been captivated by a book knows the power of the imagination to expand the mind. Such vivid sensations are evoked by a good book that reading can stimulate a thirst for knowledge, foster empathy, and encourage curiosity—all traits that develop from life experiences. It is for this reason that *Strong Souls Singing* includes literature representing such a broad range of subjects. Just as the storytelling tradition is about many stories told again and again, one to the next, reading isn't about one book, but about a lifetime of books. Not just novels, but histories, plays, biographies, and poems all tell a story from which we gain knowledge.

This is reason enough to share books with children and young adults. But there are other reasons, critical to even the very youngest child. We know the thrill of reading a picture book like *The Genie in the Jar* or *Cornrows* with a child at our side, but doing so is more than just having fun. By giving the child a chance to become familiar with the sight of words and their meanings, we're preparing him or her to flourish in school. Further, the warmth and affection of the situation teaches the child to associate those feelings with reading: a kindness that a child will never forget, and the beginnings of a love for reading that will enrich an entire life.

Along with providing a shared experience unlike any other, reading and discussing literature with the child or young adult allows you to confront difficult questions outside the heat of the experience. This makes reading with small groups of young people especially valuable; books can give you the opportunity to talk about every imaginable topic.

For teens, who are going through so many changes, having a chance to read and talk about a character or person they can relate to, like Cassie in *Roll of Thunder, Hear My Cry* or Veronica Chambers in *Mama's Girl*, can help them make sense of complex feelings. At the same time, learning about their own cultural history in *The Best of The Brownies' Book* or about others from a different time or place can give young people some perspective on their own lives, and foster a strong sense of identity. And for all readers, the sheer genius of masterworks like *The Street* or *And Still I Rise* can nurture a tremendous sense of pride.

When we engender a love for reading in our children—by bringing books into their lives, by reading to them and with them—we expand their world immeasurably.

Index of Books by Title

The Color Purple. Alice Walker. New York: Harcourt Brace Jovanovich, 1982. *92*

Cornrows. Camille Yarbrough. Illustrations by Carole Byard. New York: Coward, McCann & Geoghegan, 1979. *43*

Cousins. Virginia Hamilton. New York: Philomel Books, 1990. *49*

Devil's Gonna Get Him. Valerie Wilson Wesley. New York: G. P. Putnam's Sons, 1995. *94*

Disappearing Acts. Terry McMillan. New York: Viking, 1989. *84*

Fires in the Mirror: Crown Heights, Brooklyn and Other Identities. Anna Deavere Smith. Foreword by Cornel West. New York: Anchor Books, 1993. *25*

Flyin' West. Pearl Cleage. New York: Dramatists Play Service, 1995. *29*

for colored girls who have considered suicide / when the rainbow is enuf: a choreopoem. Ntozake Shange. New York: MacMillan, 1977. *33*

The Friends. Rosa Guy. New York: Holt, Rinehart and Winston, 1973. *61*

The Genie in the Jar. Nikki Giovanni. Illustrations by Chris Raschka. New York: Henry Holt, 1996. *122*

Get On Board: The Story of the Underground Railroad. James Haskins. New York: Scholastic, 1993. *12*

Go Down, Moses: A Celebration of the African-American Spiritual. Richard Newman. Illustrations by Terrance Cummings. Foreword by Cornel West. New York: Clarkson Potter, 1998. *17*

Going Back Home: An Artist Returns to the South. Paintings by Michele Wood. Story interpreted and written by Toyomi Igus. San Francisco: Children's Book Press, 1996. *99*

The Good Negress. A. J. Verdelle. Chapel Hill, NC: Algonquin Books of Chapel Hill, 1995. *91*

Gorilla, My Love. Toni Cade Bambara. New York: Random House, 1972. *69*

The Harlem Renaissance. Veronica Chambers. Philadelphia: Chelsea House Publishers, 1998. *11*

Harriet Tubman: Conductor on the Underground Railroad. Ann Petry. New York: Crowell, 1955. *109*

Her Stories: African American Folktales, Fairy Tales, and True Tales. Virginia Hamilton. Illustrations by Leo and Diane Dillon. New York: Blue Sky Press, 1995. *56*

Hold Fast to Dreams. Andrea Davis Pinkney. New York: Morrow Junior Books, 1995. *54*

Honey, I Love and Other Love Poems. Eloise Greenfield. Illustrations by Leo and Diane Dillon. New York: Crowell, 1978. *127*

I Hadn't Meant to Tell You This. Jacqueline Woodson. New York: Delacorte Press, 1994. *68*

I Have a Dream. Dr. Martin Luther King, Jr. Foreword by Coretta Scott King. Illustrations by fifteen Coretta Scott King Award and Honor Book Artists. New York: Scholastic, 1997. *9*

The Memphis Diary of Ida B. Wells: An Intimate Portrait of the Activist as a Young Woman. Ida B. Wells. Edited with an introduction by Miriam DeCosta-Willis. Foreword by Mary Helen Washington. Afterword by Dorothy Sterling. Boston: Beacon Press, 1995. *119*

The Middle Passage: White Ships/Black Cargo. Tom Feelings. Introduction by John Henrik Clarke. New York: Dial Books, 1995. *19*

Mojo and String: Two Plays by Alice Childress. Alice Childress. New York: Dramatists Play Service, 1971. *28*

Mother Love: Poems. Rita Dove. New York: W. W. Norton, 1995. *130*

Mufaro's Beautiful Daughters: An African Tale. Written and illustrated by John Steptoe. New York: Lothrop, Lee & Shepard Books, 1987. *45*

One of Three. Angela Johnson. Illustrations by David Soman. New York: Orchard Books, 1991. *38*

Our Song, Our Toil: The Story of American Slavery as Told by Slaves. Edited by Michele Stepto. Brookfield, CT: Millbrook Press, 1994. *15*

Passing. Nella Larsen. New York: Knopf, 1929. *81*

A Piece of Mine. J. California Cooper. Navarro, CA: Wild Trees Press, 1984. *75*

Pretty Fire. Charlayne Woodard. New York: Plume, 1995. *26*

A Raisin in the Sun: A Drama in Three Acts. Lorraine Hansberry. New York: Random House, 1959. *24*

The Road to Memphis. Mildred D. Taylor. New York: Dial Books, 1990. *72*

Roll of Thunder, Hear My Cry. Mildred D. Taylor. Frontispiece by Jerry Pinkney. New York: Dial Books, 1976. *66*

Rosa Parks: My Story. Rosa Parks and James Haskins. New York: Dial Books, 1992. *108*

Running Girl: The Diary of Ebonee Rose. Sharon Bell Mathis. San Diego: Browndeer Press, 1997. *51*

Second Daughter: The Story of a Slave Girl. Mildred Pitts Walter. New York: Scholastic, 1996. *59*

Selected Poems. Gwendolyn Brooks. New York: Harper & Row, 1963. *132*

She Dared to Fly: Bessie Coleman. Dolores Johnson. New York: Benchmark Books, 1997. *102*

The Shimmershine Queens. Camille Yarbrough. New York: G. P. Putnam's Sons, 1989. *55*

A Shining Thread of Hope: The History of Black Women in America. Darlene Clark Hine and Kathleen Thompson. New York: Broadway Books, 1998. *20*

The Sleeper Wakes: Harlem Renaissance Stories by Women. Edited and with an introduction by Marcy Knopf. Foreword by Nellie Y. McKay. New Brunswick, NJ: Rutgers University Press, 1993. *80*

Sojourner Truth: Ain't I a Woman? Patricia C. and Fredrick McKissack. New York: Scholastic, 1992. *107*

Song of the Trees. Mildred D. Taylor. Illustrations by Jerry Pinkney. New York: Dial Press, 1975. *58*

Index of Authors

Index of Books by Reading Level

Picture Books:
History: *8, 9*
Novels and Short Stories: *36-45*
Autobiography: *98, 99*
Poetry: *122-125*

Grades 1 to 3:
History: *8, 9*
Novels and Short Stories: *36-43*
Autobiography: *98, 99*
Poetry: *122, 123, 125*

Grades 4 to 5:
History: *8-12, 14*
Novels and Short Stories: *42-46, 48-52, 54-60*
Autobiography: *98-102, 104*
Poetry: *122-128*

Grades 6 to 7:
History: *8-12, 14, 15*
Novels and Short Stories: *44-46, 48-52, 54-66, 68*
Autobiography: *98-102, 104-110*
Poetry: *124-128*

Grades 8 to 9:
History: *8-12, 14-17*
Drama: *24-26*
Novels and Short Stories: *52, 54-66, 68-70, 72, 73*
Autobiography: *98, 99, 104-113*
Poetry: *125-128, 130*

Grade 10 to Adult:
History: *8, 9, 11, 12, 14-21*
Drama: *24-30, 32, 33*
Novels and Short Stories: *56-66, 68-70, 72-88, 90-95*
Autobiography: *98, 99, 105-114, 116-119*
Poetry: *125-128, 130-135*

The Givens Foundation for African American Literature

The Givens Foundation for African American Literature was established in 1972 as the Archie and Phebe Mae Givens Foundation. Its original purpose was to provide scholarships to African American students. The Foundation's focus shifted in 1985 when the Givens family worked with the Twin Cities African American community to purchase a 3,000-piece collection of African American literature—one of the most important collections of its kind in the nation. Since then, the Archie Givens Sr. Collection of African American Literature housed at the University of Minnesota Library has inspired and supported the Foundation's efforts.

Today, the mission of the Foundation is to celebrate and promote African American literature and history through programs and activities that encourage reading and increase public awareness of African American writers. The Foundation is guided by a volunteer advisory board.

Archie Givens is Director of the Givens Foundation for African American Literature. He is also editor of *Spirited Minds: African American Books for Our Sons and Our Brothers,* the companion volume to *Strong Souls Singing.*